THE SOLDIER'S LOAD

and

THE MOBILITY OF A NATION

Colonel S. L. A. Marshall

PUBLISHED BY
THE MARINE CORPS ASSOCIATION
QUANTICO, VIRGINIA

This material appeared originally in
The Infantry Journal and *The Combat Forces Journal*

Of the two score military books and manuals which I have written, this essay which first appeared in 1949 has had by far the most instructive history and consequence.

I was therefore delighted when the publishers of the new edition agreed with me that its genesis and aftermath must be made part of the story.

The basic theme is elementary and should be beyond argument: No logistical system is sound unless its first principle is enlightened conservation of the power of the individual fighter.

The secondary theme, in 1949 a radically new idea, as yet unsupported by incontrovertible scientific proof, is that sustained fear in the male individual is as degenerative as prolonged fatigue and exhausts body energy no less.

Today, this second proposition is commonly accepted in medical and military circles. As to the first proposition, we are doing better and everyone gives it lip service. But there remain too many jokers down the line who still haven't gotten the word.

About the evolution of the essay, and as to the course I ran, I am reminded of the Irishman whose horse ran last in a field of sixteen. When the animal finally passed him, he leaned over the rail and whispered: "Pray, what took you so long?"

In July, 1918, I marched with my Regiment to the front on a balmy, starlit night and was astonished to see the strong men around me virtually collapse under the weight of their packs when we got to the fire zone after an 11-mile approach on a good road. They had been conditioned to go 20 miles under the same weight in a broiling sun. Then some days later, after our bath of fire and burials were done, we shouldered the same packs, marched rearward 32 miles in one day and got to our billets with no sweat, feeling light as a feather.

I should have seen the lesson then. But to my juvenile mind the experience signified only that it is a lot easier to move away from a battle than to go into one, which any fool knows.

Many years went by. Then in the Pacific War in early 1944, Major General Archibald V. Arnold gave me a tactical problem to solve. He wished to know why it was that in the atoll operations, if troops were checked three times by fire, even though they took no losses and had moved not more than a mile, their energy was spent and they could not assault.

As is fully explained in *Men Against Fire,* I was able to advance a tactical solution for the problem, though I still could not answer his question. The mystery grew until it haunted me.

Then after Omaha Beach, as is described in this essay, I dealt with companies whose battle experience had variously gone the whole gamut from utter defeat and mass panic to preserved order under heavy pressure, and distinguished achievement. When at last my field notes were complete, they said to me that there was one truth about the nature of fear which men had missed through the ages. Still, I hesitated to speak.

In 1948 I raised the question with my personal friend, Dr. Raymond W. Waggoner, chief of psychiatry at the University of Michigan and a sage in many fields. He was at first skeptical about the theory and said that the physical effects of fear and fatigue might seem to be the same but he believed that the rebound from fear would be more rapid. When I stood on the documentation, he called in some of the biologists. They rallied to my side of the discussion, one of them saying: "We have been thinking along these lines for some years." After hearing them out, Dr. Waggoner warmed to the subject, gave me a private lesson in bio-chemistry and imparted the confidence which enabled me to proceed.

Since I am not a scientist, the organic reaction to fear is not a proper part of this statement. Such details do not stay in my mind and those who are interested in them have a plethora of learned writings to ponder. We simply found out that we were on the right track. After the theory was launched, medical laboratories in several of our main universities took it under study, and by varying tests proved it to be correct. One of them, I now recall, made its findings by examining men undergoing major dental surgery, as to the count of male sex hormones excreted through the urine before and after. Still later, during the Korean War, one of the research organizations serving the Army put scientists into the line to make comparable tests of fighters before and after combat, with general results, as I recall, doubly confirming what had already been substantially proved.

At about the same time there was a study in the University of Utah for some months to determine how long this truth had been kicking around underfoot; that is to say, that all of the basic evidence was in the hands of scientists, but none had bothered to add two and two to make four of it. I think these researchers concluded that there was no excuse for ignorance after the year 1890. If that's the wrong date (or the wrong school) it's because I kept no file on the business, feeling no interest in the experiments.

What is said in the essay concerning optimum loading the Army took seriously. One Army board set up its own test apparatus, complete with treadmill, etc., to measure human stress under assorted loads at varying distances. The Quartermaster Climatic Research Laboratory ran other parallel tests and published reports of same which continued into the late 1950s. The opening paragraph of the first study acknowledged that the research had been stimulated by this essay. From that same writing by Dr. Farrington Daniels, Jr., M. D. I quote only these words: "It is disturbing to speculate that since 1750 several hundred million men have gone into combat on foot carrying back loads, while during this time probably less than a hundred men carrying loads have been subjected to scientific study."

Programs were projected for lightening all line items which the infantryman must carry into battle. What came of all this motion in the end I cannot say. Completed data often may point to the existence of a pressing problem, but within a bureaucracy thousands of minds must be in tune to evolve the technical solution affording the bettering of a system. As Admiral A. T. Mahan said, this is the great evil.

In Korea, when the scientists were double checking the laboratory data, I was viewing off-and-on the same problem in quite another dimension, and going on to a startling tentative conclusion. Here was a unique battlefield. With its high, ubiquitous ridges, limited foregrounds, climatic extremes and short-duration fire fights, Korea gave us the best opportunity to measure combat stress that we will ever know. We took little advantage of it.

My field notes convinced me that we need to take a fresh look at the recovery interval which follows troop exhaustion. Man is better than we know; his tired body will rebound quicker than we think.

Take one example. After a wearing approach march and entrenching, two rifle companies went into perimeter on adjoining ridges. They were the same strength; the positions were about equal. Both units were dog tired. One commander ordered a 100 percent alert. The other put his men in the sacks and with a few of his NCOs kept watch. Thirty minutes later the Chinese attacked. The first company was routed and driven from its hill immediately. The second bounded from its sleeping bags, fought like tigers and held the position until finally ordered by battalion to withdraw.

Another incident is described in detail in *The River and the Gauntlet*. One company of the Wolfhound Regiment was flattened when overrun by a Chinese brigade. The unit looked utterly spent. The brigade charged on to take position atop a ridge blocking the route of withdrawal for the regiment. The stricken company, after one hour in the sacks, was ordered to take the ridge. Even before the ascent started, every company officer was felled by fire. Without a break the survivors swept the slope and carried the crest.

If these episodes mean what they say, then some of our security procedures when in the presence of the enemy need to be re-examined. Worn out men cannot fight or think. It is folly to press them beyond endurance when just a little rest will work a miracle of recovery.

A collateral proposition is best illuminated by citations from Marine operations. When the 7th Regiment emerged on the Koto-ri plateau in November, 1950, it was met with bitter cold and the first spark of enemy resistance simultaneously. Returning patrols showed every symptom of men in intense shock. Pulse rates were abnormally low. The individuals gibbered, grimaced vaguely and could not articulate. The puzzled doctors treated them empirically with a heavy shot of grog and bed rest. Eight hours later, they were normal.

On the other hand, the remnants of the 7th Division elements, which 1st Marine Division brought out over the ice of the Chosin in an heroic exploit, had been enveloped by the enemy for the greater part of one week. The cold, the privation and the suffering at the hands of the CCF had been extremely harsh throughout. In the case of these men, Major General Oliver Smith felt that at least 48 hours total rest was essential. At the end of that time, he concluded by personal inspection that the ones which had escaped wounds and frostbite could march out with the column from Hagaru-ri and do normal duty.

There is only a suggestion here that the recovery period is in ratio to the duration of the extraordinary pressure resulting in exhaustion. Appearances are not to be trusted. The unit knocked out by five hours of marching, digging and hard fighting may look no less down and dispirited than the unit saved after three days of envelopment and hand-to-hand combat on a hilltop. It does not follow that what the two require for recovery is at all alike. This subject requires far more attention than anyone has yet given it. There is more to be learned about man under pressure than we yet know and the areas for profitable research which remain unexplored are wide indeed.

One trouble is that we are slow to alter our procedures even after ordeal by fire has shown where they are at fault; this is due to the drag of orthodoxy which is a quite different thing from tradition. Another difficulty is that the practical lessons that we learn in war and apply under the gun are too often obscured in the pursuit of some other object under the conditions of peacetime training.

Two anecdotes, both dating from 1956, both bearing directly on the thoughts expressed in this essay, underscore my meaning. Israel's Army is exactly as old as is this small book. Right after publication, that Army translated the book into Hebrew and made its principles a part of operating doctrine for all troop leaders.

In the book *Sinai Victory* you will find this tale. Israel's general campaign into the Sinai wastes was to begin with a battalion attack on Queisima, not far from the oasis called Kadesh Barnea in the Bible. H-hour for the whole campaign was determined by an estimate of when this troop body would close on the position. But the night advance through the dunes and into the wadis was a killer and the men staggered and stumbled. As the battalion got to within strike range of the target village, the Commander's watch told him that he was still on time but his eyes saw just as clearly that his men were spent. He could not get in touch with the High Command by radio. Even so, he made the decision to postpone for one hour this triggering assault while his men lay down in the sands in their great coats and slept.

The contrasting episode occurred at about this same time. I had flown via Naples to join the Israeli Army in the Sinai Desert. Over a weekend I was with the Sixth Fleet off Sicily. On Monday, there was to proceed a two-battalion exercise, an attack by Marines on Sardinia, with the Navy doing its part. That Sunday morning, we gathered on the flagship and with Admirals Walter F. Boone and Charles R. (Cat) Brown present, the full-dress briefing prior to attack perforce went as smoothly as a Broadway musical in its second year.

At the end, Admiral Boone asked: "Any questions, General Marshall?"

I said: "Yes, one question. As I get it, the battalion attacking just after dawn gets in landing craft four miles out. The beach is defended at the waterline by about two companies, working heavy mortars and machine guns, along with small arms. Their bunker line is along that low-lying ridge 700 yards inland. The battalion will take that by mid-morning. It will then go on to that first high range, marked 1,500 meters, where the enemy artillery is based. By sunset these same men are supposed to assemble on the range beyond that one where they meet the battalion coming up from the west coast. Now have you told the troops that if this were war they would be doing well if that first line of low ridges were theirs by the end of the day?"

Boone was startled. He said to the two Marine commanders: "Is this true?"

They withdrew to consider the question, then returned to say: "We agree with him."

Boone asked: "Then why are we doing it this way?"

Someone replied: "Any smaller plan wouldn't give forces enough of a workout."

I said: "Fair enough. But you have not answered my question. Have you told troops, staff and everyone else that the plan is far over-extended, that operations would not have this much reach if men were fighting?"

The answer was: "No."

I said: "That's the hell of it. No one ever does. Out of such plans and exercises in peacetime, when no precautionary words are spoken, we recreate our own myths about the potential of our human forces. Then when war comes again, men who discovered the bitter truth the hard way are all gone. *Voila,* we've got to learn all over again."

There is only one way to stop such drifting. Realistic training derives only from continued study of what happens in war. No system can go far wrong if leaders at every level know what is to be expected of their people under fire and are prepared to raise practical questions when planning staffs overlook elementary precautions. The first duty of the officer is to challenge whatever seems illusory.

The Marine Corps has a classic model on which to guide. As the analyst of General Smith's operation in the frozen north, I have long felt that its salient lesson is the Commander's deliberate conservation of his men's powers under utterly adverse conditions. Though the enemy vise steadily tightened, he still rested his troops till he felt they were ready to march and fight. Each day's movement was regulated by his measure of how far the column could go, short of exhaustion. Of this care, came the big payoff to him and to his people. At Koto-ri, after the hard day's fight, he felt worn down. Then outside his tent he heard some truckers singing the Marine hymn and his heart leaped up. He had earned that great moment. A more precipitate, but less bold, leader would have started lunging from the hour when Hagaru-ri and Yudam-ni became enveloped and 1st Marine Division would never have come down the mountain to the sea.

S. L. A. Marshall
Brig. Gen. USAR-Ret.

Dherran Dhoun
Birmingham, Michigan

CONTENTS

Part I
THE MOBILITY OF THE SOLDIER

ONE-MAN LOGISTICS

STRATEGY is the art of the general. And like any other art, it requires patience to work out its basic concepts. But the odd part of it is that among higher commanders that branch of the art most apt to be treated with a broad stroke, though it calls loudest for the sketching-in of minute details, is the *logistics* of war.

Since that word has in recent years become a catchall, covering everything pertaining to the administrative and supply establishments, it is necessary that I be exact as to how I use it here. Let us therefore take the definition of Sir George Colley, who described logistics as "the scientific combination of marches, the calculation of time and distances, and of *economy* of men's powers." This is much more satisfying than anything to be found in our own dictionaries.

But when that last phase is included (and it cannot be left out) it precludes that view of logistics which sees it only as a game for the G-4s and the mathematicians—a game to be settled with loading tables, slide rules and transportation schedules.

Logistics becomes, in fact, the very core of generalship —the thing that is ever the main idea—to get military forces into a theater of war in superior strength and husband that strength until they shall prevail. Further than that, I think we can all agree this does not mean numbers of men and weapons solely. For if it did a general would be only a glorified cattle drover, and we would say of him what Col. G. F. R. Henderson wrote of General Pope: "As a tactician, he was incapable. As a strategist, he lacked imagination. He paid no attention to the physical wants of man or beast." With the general, as with anyone under that rank, the very acme of leadership comes of the ability to lift the powers of the average man-in-the-ranks to the highest attainable level and hold them there. It is therefore especially curious that there is less competent military literature on this subject—the economy of the powers of fighting men—than on any other aspect of war.

In modern armies, more is being written about *moral* value than in the preceding nineteen centuries. Yet modern works on the art of command have almost nothing to say about the economy of men's powers. It seems to be taken for granted that the introduction of the machine into warfare is tending to produce automatic solutions of the prevailing problem of how to get more fire out of fewer men. But that can only be true if men's powers before and during battle are more carefully husbanded than they have ever been. The actual fact is that men in the mass are growing weaker. The general impact of the machine on all industrial populations is to lower the stamina of the individual and make it less likely that he will develop his legs by walking and harden his back and shoulder muscles by manual toil. Until recently the most sturdy and reliable soldiers were drawn from the agricultural population. Now the drafts are filled with men from towns and cities, more than half of whom have never taken regular exercise or participated in any group game. Likewise, the machine has tremendously increased the over-all weight of war. Two hundred years ago an army could go through a campaign with what it carried in its train and on the backs of its soldiers. But in the European Theater in the last war, every soldier had to have back of him some ten tons of matériel. And the field army that had to rely on its organic transport during an extended advance found itself soon beached high and dry.

So much for change in one direction. The machine has made warfare more ponderous but has also given it greater velocity. In the other direction there has been no change at all. *For it is conspicuous that what the machine has failed to do right up to the present moment is decrease by a single pound the weight the individual has to carry in war.* He is still as heavily burdened as the soldier of 1000 years B.C.

This load is the greatest of all drags upon mobility in combat and I submit that it is not due to unalterable circumstance. It comes mainly of the failure of armies and those who control their doctrine to look into the problem. A decisive decrease in that load is possible, once we recognize that our use of the machine can be accommodated to this end. Failing that, we will not in the future make the best use of our human material.

Nothing benefits an army, or any part of it, which is not for the good of the individual at the hour he enters battle. For that reason, the whole logistical frame of the Army of the United States should develop around an applied study of the logistical capability of *one average American soldier*.

That means getting a more accurate measure of his physical and moral limitations, and of the subtle connection between these two sides of his being. It means rejecting the old dogmatic notion that by military training alone we can transform the American soldier into a cross between Superman and Buck Rogers. It means that by first enlightening ourselves, we have the main chance to bring forth the soldier more enlightened.

THE DEAD HAND

GEN. J. F. C. FULLER once said that adherence to dogma has destroyed more armies and lost more battles and lives than anything else in war. I believe this can be proved to the hilt, and that it is time to shake it. For in the future we will not be able to afford any unnecessary expenditure.

In the study called *Men Against Fire* I dealt somewhat narrowly with the problem of conserving the average man's power on the battlefield. The main theme was that the reason all movements in minor tactics tend to fall apart is that we have not rooted our tactical thinking in a sound appreciation of how the average American thinks and reacts when hostile fire comes at him.

But the case as presented there was too limited. It considered man *only* as a being who can think—who gathers moral strength from his close comrades—who needs every possible encouragement from them if he is to make clear decisions and take constructive action in the face of enemy fire.

But something should be added. On the field of battle

man is not only a thinking animal, he is a beast of burden. He is given great weights to carry. But unlike the mule, the jeep, or any other carrier, his chief function in war does not begin until the time he delivers that burden to the appointed ground.

It is this distinction which makes all the difference. For it means that the logistical limits of this human carrier should not be measured in terms of how much cargo he can haul without permanent injury to bone and muscle, but of what he can endure without critical, and not more than temporary, impairment of his mental and moral powers. If he is to achieve military success and personal survival his superiors must respect not only his intelligence but also the delicate organization of his nervous system. When they do not do so, they violate the basic principle of war, which is conservation of force. And through their mistaken ideas of mobility they achieve only its opposite.

Almost 150 years ago, Robert Jackson, then inspector general of hospitals in the British Army, put the matter thus simply: "To produce united action of bodily power and sympathy of moral affections is the legitimate object of the tactician." The desired objective could not be stated more clearly today. It is universally recognized that the secret of successful war lies in keeping men in a condition of mental alertness and physical well-being which insures that they can and will move when given a competent order.

Yes indeed! Everybody is ready to give three cheers for mobility. But when it comes to the application of the principle at the most vital point of all—the back of the soldier going into battle—the modern commander is just as liable to be wrong about it as the father of the general staff, General Scharnhorst, when he wrote these incredible words: *"The infantryman should carry an axe in case he may have to break down a door."*

Scharnhorst did not lack for company. You cannot read far into war without noting that among the great leaders of the past there has been a besetting blindness toward this subject. Either they have not deemed it worth mentioning among the vital principles of command, or their thoughts about it were badly confused.

Take Marshal Maurice de Saxe for example since his grasp of moral problems was on the whole profound. About training he wrote eloquent truths like this one, "All the mystery of combat is in the legs and it is to the legs that we should apply ourselves." But when de Saxe turned his thoughts to the problem of man's powers on the battlefield, he said: "It is needless to fear overloading the infantry soldier with arms. This will make him more steady."

Making all allowances for the more limited movements during battle and the short killing range of all weapons during the wars of de Saxe's times, it must still be conceded that on this point he sounds like an ass. Overloading has never steadied any man or made him more courageous. And such dictum runs directly counter to the principles of war and the sound leading of soldiers.

But the words are dangerous, if only because de Saxe uttered them. We too often ascribe to successful men a godlike infallibility, instead of weighing all things in the light of reason. What the Great Captains thought, succeeding generations find it difficult to forget and challenge reluctantly despite an ever-broadening human experience.

We are still troubled by commanders who do not "fear overloading the infantry soldier with arms." Rare indeed is the high commander who will fight consistently and effectively for the opposite. In fact, it is chiefly the high commanders who have laid this curse on the back of the fighting man right down through the ages. The second lieutenants have usually known better.

Take Frederick the Great. He said that a soldier should always carry three days' food. Take Napoleon. He said on St. Helena that there are five things a soldier should never be without, "his musket, his cartridge box, his knapsack, his provisions for at least four days and his pioneer hatchet." Take Scharnhorst again. He said that a soldier should carry with him, besides his arms and a three-day supply of bread, "sixty rounds of ammunition, three spare flints, a priming wire, a sponge, a worm, an instrument for taking the lock to pieces, two shirts, two pairs of stockings, rags to wrap up his feet on a march, combs, brushes, pipe-clay, black balls, needles and thread."

We can forget such details as the "worm" and the "sponge." The point is that what a soldier is required to carry into battle today is more directly related to these hoary prescriptions than to any modern survey or analysis showing what a soldier is likely to use most in combat —and what weights he could well be spared by a more foresightful planning for the use of other forms of transport.

In fact, careful research, after first revealing the historic roots of most of these elementary logistical concepts would also enable us to trace their growth right down to the present. But the researcher would look in vain for proof that they are based upon field data rather than upon a blind adherence to tradition. He would perforce conclude with Bacon that: "The logic now in use serves rather to fix and give stability to the errors which have their foundations in commonly received notions than to help the search for truth!"

Perhaps in Frederick's day it *was* necessary for a soldier to carry three days' food in his pack. Maybe when Napoleon was on the march there *was* a sound reason for upping that figure from three to four. One can even give Stonewall Jackson the benefit of the doubt for following Frederick's rule-of-thumb during his campaigns in the Valley. Though observers noted, according to Col. Henderson, that it was the habit of the troops to bolt their three rations as soon as possible and then scrounge around for more.

But why in common sense during World War II did we put infantrymen across defended beaches carrying three full rations in their packs? In other words, nine packages of K rations, weighing roughly the same number of pounds! We did it time and again in landings where "hot cargo" shipments of food were coming onto the beaches right behind the troops and almost tripping on their heels.

One package would always have been enough—*one-third of a ration*. In fact, we learned by actual survey on the battlefield that only some three per cent of the men along the combat line touched any food at all in the first day's fighing. And that water consumption was only a fifth what it became on the second day and thereafter. Such is the economy that can be achieved by virtue of a churning stomach.

But compared to this reality, we continued until the end of the war to overload our forces with food every time we staged a major attack. To understand why we did it, we must disregard field data and look into history. Some centuries ago Frederick had an idea.

THE FIRE LOAD

A MORE critical and debatable issue than the amount of rations to be carried is the weight of the fire load, since fire is the mainspring of mobility and men can't shoot with empty guns. Again the historical roots of the solution are worth remarking.

Outdoing Scharnhorst, von Moltke in his time decided that 200 rounds of ammunition was a more fitting load for the sturdy Prussian. That became the standard requirement for modern armies. Both sides used it during the Russo-Japanese War, and most armies likewise used it in World War I. So far as may now be learned, no one of any importance saw fit to question whether that figure of 200 rounds had any justification, either in tactics or logistics. In the American Army in France of 1917-18, our commanders usually adhered to the practice of requiring troops to carry a full ammunition load during the approach march, even in moving into a "quiet" sector. And in hot weather the results were brutal. We can write off the general policy with the simple statement that troops usually had to carry *ten times* as many cartridges as there was any likelihood they would use.

Following World War I, several general staffs, and particularly the French, gave some thought to the proposal that with the improvement of first-line transport through motorization it had become possible to relieve the soldier of carrying his own ammunition reserve. But these good intentions bore no tangible fruit, though in the course of World War I such weapons and equipments as the grenade, trench knife and gas mask had been added to the soldier's over-all weight.

When World War II came along, the rule-of-thumb

laid down almost a century before by Moltke still gave the infantryman blisters around his belly, though meanwhile, owing to changes in civilian transportation, the system of forward supply had undergone a transformation so revolutionary that it had become almost impossible for the combat line to run out of ammunition. Jeeps and amtracs were carrying the stuff right up to the company CPs and on to the firing line. And when they couldn't go fast enough, planes were dropping it there in bundles.

Despite this altered situation there was no relief for the human carrier. True enough, we did not follow the Moltke prescription right down to the last cartridge. But we deviated from it, not primarily to lighten the soldier's load but to make room for other types of ammunition.

For example, during the last two years of operations in the Pacific, the rifleman put across a beach generally carried eighty rounds for his M1 or carbine. This special dispensation was simply granted him that he might the better carry eight hand grenades, or in some cases five. It was presumed that in the close-in fighting he was likely to meet, five to eight grenades would give him a wider margin of safety than double the amount of his rifle ammunition.

In the event, such calculations were found to have little practical relation to what took place along the line of fire. When you examined company operations in atoll fighting in detail, it was evident that the soldier who used grenades at all was almost as rare as the man who fired as many as eighty rounds from his rifle in any one day of action. Which is to say that the load of grenades the line was required to carry did not promote either increased safety or greater fire power. Eight grenades are a particularly cumbersome burden. They weigh 10.48 pounds. Had the grenade load of each man been cut by three-quarters (giving him two grenades) it is a reasonable assumption that the over-all and expedient tactical use of that weapon would not have been reduced, and the force so lightened would not have been made more vulnerable.

With all hands carrying eight grenades, the number of men making *any use of that weapon at all* was consistently less than six per cent of the total in any general action. Research showed further that the grenade was rarely put to any practical use in the initial stage of an amphibious attack. This was also true in Europe.

Having been a grenadier in the Army before I became qualified at anything else, I have a natural sentimental fondness for the grenade. In the First World War, I was convinced that the throw as taught was bad for American practice, and therefore conducted the first experiments that resulted in its change. But at that time I learned that if the weapon is to be employed usefully, it must be understood that a definite penalty is attached to over-estimating its usefulness. That still applies. The high command falls into such an error when it overloads the man. The soldier himself makes the error—as we learned in too many cases—when he uses the grenade to clean out the unseen interiors of such places as underground air-raid shelters and thick-walled blockhouses, and then takes it for granted the job is tactically finished.

I agree that there are conditions of terrain, and situations that involve movement through entrenchments or against houses, where the grenade is all but indispensable. But common sense says also that if it is mobility we want, there is no more justification for loading men with grenades they are not likely to use than to send them forward burdened with so many sticks and stones. In fact, that might be better, for they would then drop off their ballast at the earliest possible moment.

This same argument would eliminate altogether any further issuing of the bayonet. That weapon ceased to have any major tactical value at about the time the inaccurate and short-range musket was displaced by the rifle. But we have stubbornly clung to it—partly because of tradition which makes it inevitable that all military habits die a slow death, but chiefly because of the superstition that the bayonet makes troops fierce and audacious, and therefore more likely to close with the enemy.

I doubt that any combat officer of the last war below field grade would agree that this idea has any merit whatever. Their observations are to be trusted more than the most positive opinions of any senior commander who has had no recent experience with infighting.

The bayonet is not a chemical agent. The mere possession of it will not make men one whit more intrepid than they are by nature. Nor will any amount of bayonet *training* have such an effect. All that may be said of such training is that, like the old Butts Manual, its values derive only from the physical exercise. It conditions the mind only in the degree that it hardens the muscles and improves health.

The bayonet needs now to be re-evaluated by our Army solely on what it represents as an instrument for killing and protection. That should be done in accordance with the record, and without the slightest sentiment. So considered, the bayonet will be as difficult to justify as the type of slingshot with which David slew Goliath. A situation arose during the siege of Brest in August 1944, when the 29th Infantry Division found that an improvised slingshot *was* useful in harassing the enemy. And about all that may be said for the bayonet, too, is that there is always a chance of its being used to advantage. But the record shows that that chance is extremely slight.

In the Pacific fighting of World War II, more men were run through by *swords* than by bayonets.

In our European fighting there is only one bayonet charge of record. That was the attack by the 3d Battalion, 502d Parachute Infantry, at the Pommerague Farm during the advance on Carentan, France, in June 1944. In that attack three of the enemy were actually killed by American bayonets. It is a small irony, however, that these killings took place about six minutes after the main charge had subsided. And it is a somewhat larger irony that the one junior officer who actually closed with the bayonet and thrust his weapon home was subsequently relieved because he was not sufficiently bold in leading his troops.

AIRBORNE EXAMPLE

SINCE we are talking about mobility, and how to control the loading of the soldier toward that end, there is no chapter from our past more instructive than our airborne operations of World War II.

In the European Theater, the basic individual ammunition load for the paratrooper was eighty rounds for his carbine or M1, and two hand grenades. When the paratrooper jumped into Normandy on June 6, 1944, he also carried these things: 1 rifle and carrier part, 1 English mine, 6 packages of K-ration, 1 impregnated jump suit, 1 complete uniform, 1 steel helmet and liner, 1 knitted cap, 1 change of underwear, 2 changes of sox, 1 entrenching tool, 1 gas mask, 1 first-aid pack, 1 spoon, 2 gas protective covers, 1 field bag with suspenders, 1 packet of sulfa tablets, 1 escape kit, and a set of toilet articles.

Despite all that weight, the most salient characteristic in operations by these forces was without doubt the high mobility of all ranks. That was because most of them used common sense. They jumped heavy but they moved light. Once on the ground, most of them ditched every piece of equipment they considered unnecessary. They did this without order, and often before they had engaged any of the enemy or joined up with any of their comrades. It was a reflex to a course of training which had stressed that the main thing was to keep going.

The mainspring to the movement of these forces lay in the spirit of the men. They moved and hit like light infantry, and what they achieved in surprise more than compensated for what they lacked in fire power.

Further, at every point they pressed the fight hard, and the volume of fire over the whole operation proved to be tactically adequate, though supply remained generally adverse.

The 82d and 101st Divisions jumped into one situation where for two days all their elements were engaged by the enemy and only those groups fighting close to Utah Beach had an assured flow of ammunition. Some of the groups got additional ammunition from bundles dropped either by the initial lift or by resupply missions. But until the airborne front was passed through by the seaborne forces, many of these riflemen were completely dependent on the ammuniiton they had jumped into Normandy with—eighty rounds and two grenades.

Yet in the whole show, covering the five days of operation down to the crossing of the Merderet by the 82d and the capture of Carentan by the 101st, there is only one instance of a detachment having to yield ground temporarily because it ran short of ammunition. That happened at Le Port Bridge near the mouth of the Douve River where for three days 84 men of the 506th Parachute Infantry, under Capt. Charles G. Shettle, made one of the most courageous stands of the invasion. Their stand had the greatest strategic consequence, since this was the bridgehead where V and VII Corps were to ultimately link.

In the beginning Shettle's group survived without any loss of morale the temporary embarrassment caused by lack of ammunition. They simply fell back to the near side of the bridge. In the end they retrieved another ammunition bundle or two and recovered the lost ground.

All that happened to Shettle and his men deserves to be taken at face value. If, act by act, we could weigh out our whole infantry experience from the last war, we would discover a frequent repetition of the lesson of this small incident.

The moral is that we spend a great part of our time worrying about the wrong things.

Fundamentally there are two reasons for the chronic tendency to load the soldier down with too much ammunition rather than take the opposite chance.

No. 1 is the belief that it is good for his battle morale —that he is less likely to fight vigorously if harassed by the thought that his ammunition is running short.

This is a psychological fallacy. Soldiers' minds simply do not work that way.

The willing fighter will spend his last round if convinced that the tactical situation requires it. And he will then look around to see where he can get some more ammunition.

No. 2 is the equally fallacious belief that ammunition shortages have often been a cause of tactical disarrangement in past wars, and are therefore to be avoided at all costs. It is hard to prove historically that this is untrue, because the history of all past wars becomes pretty blurred when it attempts to focus on the firing line.

But the closer we look at the details of the fire fight in World War II, the clearer it becomes that in the conditions of modern warfare, *defeat because of an ammunition shortage is among the things least likely to happen.* The mobility of supply and the reticulation of communications make it a minimum hazard. Further, there are always reserves at hand. The soldier who is always willing and eager to use his weapons has a reserve in the duty belt of the man next him who will go along into battle *but will not fire.* Likewise, the hard-pressed unit has an ammunition reserve on one or both of its flanks, since pressure is never distributed evenly along the length of a front and it is a responsibility of the less heavily engaged to make their supply available to the forces carrying the fight.

Possibly these ideas appear theoretical and impractical. The fact remains that some of our most creditable operations have been sustained in just this manner. The principle of borrowing and sharing kept the defense alive during the defense of Bastogne. The defense, during the "eight days" of the encirclement, was on short supply for nearly all weapons. And all concerned knew it.

And though Brig. Gen. Anthony C. McAuliffe kept banging on VIII Corps' door and repeating that his lines were in danger of being overrun because of his ammunition shortage (a condition gradually eased by the air resupply missions) there was no operation of the last war in which American troops fought with higher morale and confidence. The marches were not pushed the less forcefully because many men were weaponless and munitionless until they were within a mile or two of the enemy. The action of the artillery was not less intrepid and decisive because the guns were down to ten or twelve rounds per day. We miss some of the most important implications of Bastogne if we fail to weigh these facts in proportion and relate them to the largest problems of operating field forces with maximum economy.

To save the bone and muscle of soldiers toward the preservation of their fighting powers is probably as desirable an object as any we can seek to give us greater efficiency in the future.

But we have scarcely begun to move in that direction. There is still no general awareness that the human carrier, like his former army mate, the mule, has a logistical limit, which if exceeded, will inevitably cause a loss of supply and mobility, and may produce complete breakdown.

In fact we have always done better by a mule than by a man. We were careful not to load the mule with more than a third his own weight. And the mule, so far as we know, was never a bundle of nerves. Unlike man, he never reacted to battle as did Belshazzar to the writing on

19

the wall "so that the joints of his loins were loosed and his knees smote one against the other."

The problem, and the conditions that call for a modern solution of it, were imaginatively stated to me by Gen. J. F. C. Fuller in a recent letter: "The soldier cannot be a fighter and a pack animal at one and the same time, any more than a field piece can be a gun and a supply vehicle combined. The idea is wrong at the start. Yet it is always being repeated.

"Fundamentally only two great novelties have come out of recent warfare. They are: (1) mechanical vehicles, which relieve the soldier of equipment hitherto carried by him; (2) air supply, which relieves the vehicle of the road.

"Machine guns are only quick fire and the atomic bomb is only a big bang—both are new only in quantity power and effect. But the above two novelties are of a new quality altogether so far as supply is concerned. It was only toward the end of World War II that the possible impact of these developments on future warfare was conclusively revealed."

THE WAY OF WASTAGE

TO REFRESH our minds on certain of the portents of World War II, we might also think back to the beachheads. What is the lasting impression?

A scene of terrible litter, in which waste is even more apparent than confusion. The disorder is heightened by the presence of the dead and the waiting wounded. The loosely assembled supply dumps while they are forming always look as if a great storm had just passed through.

But to the eye trained to see through this seeming chaos and note the beginnings of a system, these things are routine. They will be there in any build-up in the face of the enemy. The more dismaying spectacle is the wastage of personal supply, the vast amount of packs, weapons and ammunition tossed away by troops already moving inland in search of the enemy.

There is nothing new or novel in these sights. You saw the same kind of wastage on the field of World War I, particularly in the Argonne where the pressure was almost unremitting. Eyewitnesses reported it of Gettysburg, saying, too, that of the thousands of rifles thrown away by soldiers, by far the greater number had never been fired. Of Cold Harbor, one witness reported: "Seeing what had been thrown away, I wondered how the battle had been fought." Probably there is no other characteristic more common to all the fields on which armies have contended than this one—inexplicable waste of essential equipment.

Yet it is strangely the fact that little thought has been directed toward this aspect of war by anyone, other than simply to note that it happens. The omission may be partly due to the circumstance that we conclude too easily that we cannot control it. At the top, where there are relatively few men who have ever carried sixty-five pounds into combat, there is a disposition to charge off this kind of wastage, saying that it is part of war's necessary expense, caused largely by the men in the ranks who are duty shirkers by nature.

While there is some substance for this belief, it is still only a segment of a large and more disturbing truth. So long as we continue to tell troops that mobility is indispensable to success in battle, and preach that "safety lies forward," the most willing man who ever wore a soldier suit will discard a weight he finds he cannot carry under the extraordinary stresses of battle. If, in addition to being willing, he is also intelligent, he will make that decision at once when the moment arrives that his only alternative is to surrender to his own physical weakness and quit the fight.

But this is one of the hardest decisions the dutiful soldier is ever called on to make. It is so for the reason that by the time the decision becomes necessary, *his physical condition is likely to be such that he cannot think clearly*. Many will say, I know, looking back to their own experience in battle, that troops learned automatically to discard the things they did not need, and that therefore there is no problem. That may be true. But they only gained this kind of wisdom by hard experience, and it is invariably in the *first* battle that the greatest damage is done. About three-fourths of our combat fatigue cases were broken the first time they went into action.

If those who have thoroughly observed the nature of the battlefield cannot accept the thought that the derelict soldier is alone the great waster of matériel, then it must follow that the fault lies rearward. That the troops are the victims of bad loading and faulty estimates of the relationship of loading to soundness in tactics. When troops do not perform as expected there is always a good reason, and to charge it to human slothfulness is itself slothful thinking.

> *There can be true economy of men's powers in war only when command reckons with man as he is and not as it would like him to be.*

That, then, is the root of the difficulty. At planning levels there has always been a general ignorance of the logistical limits of the human carrier under fire, and of the drag on tactics which comes of weighting him too heavily.

HISTORY OF THE PROBLEM

WHAT is needed is a modern cure for a problem as ancient as the history of war. The historical antecedents have been well set forth by the Hygiene Advisory Committee of the British Army, which in the 1920's researched the subject of how soldiers have been loaded through the centuries, and published its findings in a pamphlet called *The Load Carried by the Soldier*. J. F. C. Fuller was a member of that commission, and it was from discussing the subject with him at about the time our forces went into Normandy that my attention was first drawn forcibly to the problem.

The work of the commission was scholarly though unimaginative. Other than establishing the direct connection between the excessive weights men carry in war and the high incidence of heart disease, kidney complaints, ailments of the circulatory system and the lungs, and augmented blood pressure among veterans, it drew no medical conclusions. It did not trace a connection between overloading and mental and physical collapse in battle. The report was not refreshed by combat data from World War I which would have contributed to knowledge of the psycho-organic changes occurring in men under fire as the consequence of being too heavily weighted. It is probable that no such information was available to the British Army, or to any other at that time. There are many areas of combat knowledge we have hardly begun to explore, and we are informed least of all about the nature of the combat line.

But what the commission did show clearly was that generals in all ages have been no respecters of the limitations of the human animal, either in or out of combat. In this they have been consistent, from Marcus Aurelius down to Marshal Montgomery. The Roman legionary, recruited usually at twenty and selected from the peasantry on a basis of sturdy strength rather than height, carried eighty pounds on his body when he went marching on the smooth Roman roads.

Though that seems brutal, we should at least add the footnote that 2,000 years after the Legion, the American Army dropped men from Higgins boats and onto the rough deep sands of Normandy carrying more than eighty pounds.

The French soldier at the time of the Crimean War carried an equipment of seventy-two pounds. The British Redcoats carried eighty pounds when they stormed our Bunker Hill. At Waterloo British infantrymen carried sixty to seventy pounds, the French about fifty-five.

Our infantry carried weights comparable to these during World War I. Conditioning soldiers to march with the heavy pack (about sixty pounds) was a training requirement. In combat more rations and munitions were added and very little of the training load was eliminated, at least by official order.

The commission found that with few exceptions, the armies of the past had honored the principle that lightness of foot in the individual produced buoyancy in the attack more in the breach than the observance.

Philip of Macedon was a notable exception. He achieved his mobility around a light infantry—the hypaspistes.

Oliver Cromwell made his Roundheads fast of foot by reducing their equipment to less than forty pounds.

Stonewall Jackson created an infantry which maneuvered fast by keeping the individual working load to a minimum. His men did not carry extra clothing, overcoats or knapsacks. They marched with rifles, ammunition and enough food to keep going. Each man carried one blanket or rubber sheet; he slept with a comrade for extra warmth. The cooking was done at a common mess with frying pans and skillets. The skillet handle was spiked so that on the march it could be stuck in a rifle barrel.

The commission found that in general, armies through the past 3,000 years have issued equipment to the soldier averaging between fifty-five and sixty pounds, and have tried to condition him to that weight by long marching.

Finally, it reached the absolute conclusion that *not in excess of forty to forty-five pounds* was a tolerable load for an average-sized man on a road march. More specifically, it stated that on the march, for training purposes, the optimum load, including clothing and personal belongings, is one-third of body weight. Above that figure the cost of carrying the load rises disproportionately to the actual increment of weight.

These were the main points. However, the commission mildly suggested that there might be a radical difference between the weight-carrying ability of a soldier on a march, where he is thinking only of putting one foot in front of the other, and his limits in a fight—where his life depends on his quick wit. It raised an eyebrow at the military thinkers for never having given serious consideration to that probability.

Necessarily then, we must go on beyond the commission's work, if there is to be any better conclusion than that simply because the Romans and Hoplites did it, it is good enough for us today.

In the material given on page 25 I am following what the British paper says about the weight carried by the Roman legionary. There is reason to think, however, that the British research was in error on this finding. My friend and colleague, Col. Hugh M. Cole, has checked most of the ancient sources on this subject and has been guided largely by the reasoning and conclusions of Delbrueck, the great German military historian. Delbrueck worked according to the principle that what the sources said about operations should be challenged if they did not square with "physical possibility"; this means applying to history the same rule by which we measured the phenomena of the battlefield in Europe and Central Pacific, and which I now say should be applied to all that we do logistically. Delbrueck was well acquainted with the German test marches of 1896 and what they indicated as to the limits of men's powers. He held that the Roman Legion must have operated within these weight limits, else it would have been impossible to explain its extraordinary mobility. Even this was a generous conclusion, since we know now that the Mediterranean man of that period was smaller in weight and in frame than modern man. Working with a seminar of German officers, Delbrueck found that many of the classical texts had been misinterpreted, as to what they purported to say about the Legion's weight-carrying ability. As one example, Livy's text had been corrupted from "supply for a few days" to "supply for 30 days", this referring to the rations carried by one man. And again, the much cited single reference to a man load of 80 pounds refers to a specific punishment march, like the British sand bag drill. By the time he had completed his research, Delbrueck had decided that the legion-ary carried only his arms, an iron ration and a stake, used for fortify-ing the camp. Such things as hand-mills, cooking utensils, tentage and entrenching tools were carried in the trains. In other words, it was soundness in logistics, and lightness in the individual, which made the Legion the most mobile force the world has ever known. The Roman carried so little excess into battle that he was able to engage in bodily physical combat, man to man, for an entire day. No foot formations since have ever marched as far and fought as many battles in so short a time as did the veteran legions at the height of Roman power. And the secret of their mobility as a force came of that exquisite combination of discipline and economy which kept the Roman individual light of foot and united to his comrades. By a series of calculations which need not be here explained, Colonel Cole has concluded that the individual weights carried within the legions were as follows:

Total for road marching............................57.2 lbs.
Total for approach march....................44 lbs.
Tactical load in combat zone..................33 lbs.

THE LIGHT THAT FAILED

AT least one serious attempt was made in the modern British Army to cope with the problem though in the end the effort was wholly frustrated. When shortly after the close of World War I, Captain B. H. Liddell Hart was called in to recast the Infantry Training Manual, he felt very strongly about the need for lightening the infantryman's load, and was given the backing of General Maxse, who had been inspector-general of training in the last year of the war. Hart went to the Small Arms School to work on his doctrine for infantry weapons, and there found in General Dalby, the assistant commandant, a man who was ardent for the same idea. Many experiments took place, accompanied by demonstrations of what an infantryman, stripped for action like an athlete, would look like, and how quickly he could move. The ranks developed a tremendous enthusiasm for these ideas.

Then unfortunately a slump set in and the question was postponed. To some extent the simultaneous struggle for the development of mobile armored forces tended to obscure the need for making the foot soldier more mobile. Leading advocates of tank warfare were inclined to argue that the reform of infantry equipment did not matter, as tanks would dominate the future battlefield and leave little place for infantry. When in 1925, the new Chief of the Imperial General Staff Designate, General Milne (an artilleryman by origin) became a convert to armor, he went so far as to say that it would be a waste of time and effort to make the infantry more mobile. Subsequently, Milne began to shy away from armor, despite the efforts of J. F. C. Fuller to hold him to the mark. In fact, Milne's influence on British theories of warfare appears to be noteworthy only as a depressing example of the chief, who having reached the top rung of the ladder, is all too ready to forget everything that really counts on the field of war.

Despite many of the criticisms of Hart, coming mainly from those who between wars bothered to read only partway into his theories, history will credit him with being, in the period between World Wars, Britain's most indefatigable opponent of the closed military mind. Eventually there was a revival of interest in his idea that infantry had to be given a new mobility. General Campbell (a cavalryman) was in command at Aldershot. Influenced by Hart's book on W. T. Sherman, he undertook to carry out tests of how equipment of every kind could be lightened—in the division as a whole, as well as in the infantry unit. On his proposal, the General Staff agreed that the training season of 1931 at Aldershot should be devoted to what was called a "Sherman March," looking to the lightening of the burden of field forces. It produced some startling results, pointing to a general conclusion that all of the combat arms were victims of over-loading.

That autumn the General Staff was moved to order the creation of committees in all principal commands to extend the Aldershot experiments. Hart became a general consultant. All of the reports were highly progressive and drastic. The most forward-looking came from the Aldershot Committee, where Dalby had moved in as President. Its detailed recommendations brought the total weight of the soldier's clothing, arms, ammunition and equipment (including rations and water) down to 31 lbs., 10 oz.

The following year extensive trials were carried out by the Army during the annual maneuvers by formations carrying a much reduced scale of equipment. While the reduction could not be carried quite as far as had been recommended, because that depended on the manufacture of various new items of equipment, the load was brought down to 34 lbs. in some brigades and to 35 lbs. in others.

When World War II came along, the very practical nature of these experiments and their conclusions became forgotten, and the load started creeping up again, because of abnormal staff pressures and fears, and the general failure of the Army to lay a sound logistical basis for the reform during the period of peacetime training.

FEARS OF THE STAFF

IF A YOUNG and inexperienced company commander is ignorant about what happens to men so heavily loaded they have no fair chance for movement and survival in combat, he will not ruin the army. The probability is that he will not even hurt his own company. Some higher-up, with a slightly wiser head, will straighten him out.

But when a staff is ignorant on this subject, then woe to the fighting line! The damage will not be undone, for a price will certainly be paid. This truth was repeatedly proved during World War II. We killed men unnecessarily because of our faulty appreciation of this.

The staff tended always to load the combat soldier according to its own view of every possible emergency that might confront him. With every member of a staff trying hard to think of every possible contingency, and no one above the staff enforcing a rigid weight limit to protect the soldier's back, the loads frequently became unsupportable.

With what results? The excess weights were simply not moved forward, mobile fire power was smothered. The combat line faltered and sometimes foundered under bangalore torpedoes that were never exploded, gas equipment that was never used and ropes for scaling that might have proved useful had the battalion landed next to a cliff. The inertia thus begun was increased farther down the line by commanders who permitted their men to be killed with kindness instead of firmly insisting that they make the weight required for the contest.

These twin evils were subject to control. Our tactical power and general battle efficiency could have been increased had we:

(1) Established an absolute weight limit for men in combat.

(2) Enforced it by a rigid system of inspection.

We did neither. In this one particular, we acted less wisely than the ancient Scots who at Bannockburn went into battle with each fighting man feeling as light as air because his weapon had been carried up to battle by a porter. (It is of record that the battle turned on this fact. The English saw the mob of porters moving over Gillies Hill, mistook it for a fresh reinforcing army, and fled the field.)

We should take a somewhat more careful look at the detail of this overloading, if only to realize how silly we can get under the press of active operations. Going to France in World War I, a Marine officer was advised to carry along 1 bedding roll, pillow and mattress, 1 clothing roll, 2 blankets, 1 overcoat, 2 blouses winter field, 2 trousers winter field, 2

31

breeches winter field, 1 coat sweater, 4 flannel shirts, 2 cravats, 1 small rubber boots, 1 hip rubber boots, 3 pairs shoes with extra laces, 1 high lace leather boots, 3 pair shoes with extra laces, 1 high lace leather boots, 1 puttees spiral, 1 puttees leather, 1 cap, 1 campaign hat, 2 khaki coats, 2 khaki trousers, 1 canvas leggings, 2 khaki breeches, 12 handkerchiefs olive drab, 2 wrist watches, 1 note book, 2 pajamas woolen, 1 canvas bucket, 1 rubber sponge, 1 thermos bottle unbreakable, 1 nest aluminum cups, 1 poncho, 1 housewife, 3 pillow cases, 4 sheets, 6 socks heavy, 6 sicks light, 4 suits underwear heavy woolen, 6 suits underwear light woolen, 6 suits underwear light summer, 2 garters, 2 belly bands, 1 Romeo slippers, 4 towels face, 2 towels bath, 2 soap face, 2 soap shaving, 2 tooth brushes, 2 toothpaste, 1 raincoat, 1 bathrobe, 1 manicure set, 1 set of brushes, 1 polished mirror, 1 knife, 1 compass, 1 whistle, 1 field glass, 1 leather gloves buckskin, 1 jar tobacco with pipes and water-tight matchbox, 1 amber glasses, 1 can opener and corkscrew, 1 Elliott ear protector, 1 flashlight with extra batteries. The official memorandum adds somewhat brightly that in addition to FSR, the officer should carry along whatever books he thinks he might need.

But the Marines did better as they went along. In Pacific operations throughout World War II, they outstripped the Army in getting down to the bare essentials.

When the 153rd Infantry Regiment went staggering ashore against the supposedly Japanese-held base at Kiska in the Aleutians, it was an A-1 exhibit, not of fighting power, but of how the uncontrolled fears of the staff are sometimes permitted to destroy the mobility of fighting bodies. Its load requirements was so extraordinary that members of the Regiment preserved the list that in later years they might boast of the unusual trials of soldiers to their disbelieving civilian friends. This was what each man carried:

Underwear	240 rounds ammo	Flashlight
Shirt (w/o tie)	Rifle	Maps
Kersey lined	Pack board	Pocketknife
trousers	Sleeping bag	Change of clothing
Alaskan field jacket	2 shelter halves,	Wire cutters
Helmet, steel	pole & pins	Waterproof
Helmet liner	12 cans C rations	matchbox
Raincoat	Heat tablets	Identification panel
Poncho	Cook stove	Ruck sack
Extra shoes	2 cans sterno	4 chocolate bars
Rifle belt	Long knife	3 signal panels
6 grenades	Intrenching tool	Compass
	Bayonet	

And just to make things rosey all around and keep this mule train in good spirits, the last item on the list was "Book of Battle Songs." One lieutenant of infantry who went ashore with 153rd pronounced the only judgment possible on this stupendous piece of folly: "Had the enemy been there with only two machine guns, we would have been repelled; had we landed in a fighting situation, we could not have advanced one foot."

Yet there were also instances in the Pacific war of the American staff officer advocating a bold solution of this problem, and by submitting his reasoning to battle proof, providing an example which all others can well afford to remember.

Just prior to the invasion of Aitape by Task Force 705, Lieut. Col. H. C. Brookhart loaded himself with everything which the order had said that the line infantryman was to carry during the landing.

The burden, exclusive of helmet and uniform, weighed approximately 46 pounds. Thus decked out, Brookhart presented himself to the commander, Brig. Gen. Jens Anderson Doe.

"What in hell have you got on?" asked Doe.

"This," replied Brookhart, "is what we say should be in the rifleman's load."

"Then for God's sake get rid of part of it!"

So instructed, Brookhart cut back the load to include the following items:

change of underwear	light woolen sweater
handkerchief	2 canteens of water
extra socks	aid pack
2/3 of one ration	rifle
poncho	30 rounds of rifle ammo.

He arranged that troops would put into a B-bag these items—mess gear, change of shoes, remainder of ration, clean uniform, change of underwear, change of socks—which would be brought forward by first-line transports. Toilet articles had been included in the packload. Otherwise, this was all that the line formations carried.

Brookhart kept careful check of the results of this experiment. Looking back at it, he felt that he might have risked halving the ammo load which was hand-carried. His check showed that only a minor number of riflemen had expended as many as 15 rounds on the first day.

LESSONS FROM OMAHA

IN THE INITIAL ASSAULT waves at Omaha Beachhead there were companies whose men started ashore, each with four cartons of cigarettes in his pack—as if the object of operations was trading with the French.

Some never made the shore because of the cigarettes. They dropped into deep holes during the wade-in, or they fell into the tide nicked by a bullet. Then they soaked up so much weight they could not rise again. They drowned. Some were carried out to sea but the greater number were cast up on the beach. It impressed the survivors unforgettably—that line of dead men along the sands, many of whom had received but trifling wounds. One man said of this sight: "They looked like wax: I thought of Madame Tussaud's."

There are no final death statistics on Omaha. If any are in time published, they will be at best a rough approximation. No one can say with authority whether more men died directly from enemy fire than perished because of the excess weight that made them easy victims of the water.

But when I had concluded my work with the survivors of the companies which had landed during the initial Omaha assault, the impression was inescapable that weight and water—directly or indirectly—were the cause of the greater part of our losses at the beach.

Believing that this was the great lesson of the Omaha operation, and that it was more strongly illuminated there than in other landings during World War II because of the decisiveness of that operation and the numbers engaged, I feel that the tactical facts deserve even closer scrutiny than those questions of higher strategy on which we differed with the British or among ourselves.

The fundamental error was a simple one. We overestimated the physical strength of men in the conditions of combat. This almost cost us the beachhead. Since it is the same kind of mistake that armies and their commanders have been making for centuries, there is every reason to believe it will happen again.

The mistake can be blamed only in part on the staff. In war our treatment of any basic problem reflects in large measure our thinking on the same problem during peace. It was so in this case. The general correctives needed could only have been applied by concrete thinking on the problem well in advance of war.

The root of the trouble lies here. We do lip service to the principle that the aim in logistics is not simply to support and supply the men on the fire line, but to relieve them of all unnecessary strain and tension. But it is lip service only.

We are reluctant to believe *absolutely* that 5,000 relatively fresh fighting men will defeat 15,000 worn-out men in the opposing line any day in the week.

In the hour of decision, the strength of an army cannot be counted in bodies but in the numbers of men who are spiritually willing and physically able to pick up and move on forward fighting.

At Omaha Beachhead our count of such men was extremely low. Certainly fear of death played a part in the paralysis of some of the men who couldn't get over the sands. However, we would be selling short our own human material, and would once again be guilty of gross ignorance about the underlying causes of terror among men who fight, if we took it for granted that the only reason so many men collapsed at Omaha was because they had to go through bullet and shell fire once they hit the shore.

To say that they would all have made it had they landed on a dry run exercise doesn't mean a thing.

EYEWITNESS ACCOUNT

O N D-DAY, Capt. Richard F. Bush landed with the assault waves at Omaha Beach. He was a field artilleryman. He went in on the same mission as the late Lieut. Col. "Moon" Mullins, one of the immortals of that great undertaking. Their task was to prepare the way for the landing of their own guns. But the guns didn't arrive. Again, someone's excess caution defeated the end in view. The guns were to be brought in on DUKWs. But somebody decided that the DUKWs and their cargo would be vulnerable to fire from the shore. So each DUKW was protected with a rampart of eighteen sandbags. Between this weight and the roughness of the water, every gun save one was drowned at sea.

So it was that Bush and Mullins spent their morning trying to persuade demoralized infantrymen to resume their duty. Mullins was killed while trying to lead friendly tanks against German pillboxes punishing the American flanks. There is no braver story in our history than the action of this one man on that particular morning.

This is what Bush—Mullins's companion—said of the men among whom he moved: "They lay there motionless and staring into space. They were so thoroughly shocked that they had no consciousness of what went on. Many had forgotten they had firearms to use. Others who had lost their arms didn't seem to see that there were weapons lying all around them. Some could not hold a weapon after it was forced into their hands. Others, when told to start cleaning a rifle, simply stared as if they had never heard such an order before. Their nerves were spent and nothing could be done about them. The fire continued to search for them, and if they were hit, they slumped lower into the sands and did not even call out for an aid man."

Words almost identical with these were written by Captain Hoenig back during the Franco-Prussian War. He had seen the rout of the Prussian 38th Brigade on the field of Mars-la-Tour. It had lost fifty-three per cent of its strength in a few hours. He noted of the survivors that their eyes stared but saw nothing, and if their ears heard they conveyed no message to the brain. He said of them: "I saw madness in these men, the madness that arises *from bodily exhaustion combined with the most abject terror.*"

It is unfortunate that such scenes from war are rarely understood in their full significance. Among soldiers, it is traditional to think of this condition of acute battle-field shock as occurring in a body of men only after a terrible defeat, when all hope is fled. From such a superficial conclusion can be drawn no more profitable moral than that in war, as elsewhere, it is prudent always to be on the winning side.

Because there is much more than that to be learned, I turn back to my original notes on the operation at Omaha Beachhead for values which received only passing notice in the official published account, although that account was based on these same notes.

This one passage tells a small part of what happened to Company E of the 16th Infantry, on the morning of June 6, 1944:

Altogether the company lost 105 men during the day. But of that number, only one man was killed during the advance from the top of the beach inland. Most of the others were lost in the water. Many who were wounded on leaving the boats got only as far as the edge of the sand. They collapsed there and were overtaken and drowned by the tide, which moved at the pace of a man in a slow walk. In attempting to save some of these men, others were knocked down by enemy fire, and they too were drowned by the tide. The wounding of a man at the water's edge usually meant his death.

The company line, on leaving the boats, halted just beyond the water, and the men immediately dropped to the sand. Sergeants Fitzsimons, Ellis and Toth, among others, tried to rally the line and get it to move forward. They realized, they said, that they were in a death trap and that the only way to save the company was to get it across the beach.

And so the leaders shouted to the men. But on arising they found that they were stopped by their own physical weakness. The three sergeants said that after dragging themselves forward a few steps at a time, they had to drop because their legs wouldn't support them. They said, also, that they and the others would probably have remained inert had not the tide kept moving behind them so that they had to advance to escape being drowned.

Fitzsimons saw two of his men—Privates Walch and Spencer—drop onto the sand, and saw their bodies blown into the air again. They had been killed outright by dropping on mines. Such incidents did not affect the halting pace of the company. It continued to go forward at the speed of the tide until the high-water mark was reached. There for a time it halted.

Though the company lost more men to the water behind it than to the fire from in front, it required one hour to cross 250 yards of beach.

These facts were established at a company critique which included all surviving witnesses. What went into the record was read to the company for their free comment. It therefore comprises as accurate a statement as is within human means. Many of the men were seasoned veterans, already accustomed to the sights and sounds of combat. Without doubt, heavy shock, resulting from unusually hard initial losses, was partly responsible for their semiparalyzed advance.

And that is the point! Through research conducted during World War II, our medical service now knows more about the effects of battle shock, and somewhat more of the causes, than men have ever known before. But I would point out that this knowledge will never be of general utility to the Army so long as it is considered a subject primarily of interest to the psychiatrists. What is requisite is that the branches which deal with tactics become equally well informed about the root causes of shock—instead of remaining satisfied with the narrow view that it occurs in some men "because they don't know how to take it." Only so can we apply preventive medicine.

The heart of the lesson is that *all men* feel shock in battle in some degree. It will vary from man to man, according to the intensity of each man's fear. And from situation to situation, according to the measure of success or failure felt by most of those directly concerned. But in one important respect, its consequences do not vary.

In the measure that the man is shocked nervously, and that fear comes uppermost, he becomes physically weak. His body is drained of muscular power and of mental coordination.

For these reasons, every extra pound he carries on his back reduces all of his tactical capabilities.

This being the case, we are moving only through the kindergarten of leadership when we speak of troops becoming "mentally pinned" by a low combat morale. That is, unless we are willing to accept the other half of it—that they may also become "morally pinned" by the faulty logistics of their superiors.

THE WEAKNESS OF THE STRONG

I T IS ELEMENTARY that there can be no true economy of men's powers on the battlefield unless there is respect for the natural physical limitations of the average individual. But since it appears radical in that it undercuts the traditional belief that by encouraging men to think brave thoughts we can stimulate them to endeavors they scarcely dream of, some further illustration is required. It is provided by the experience of Company M, 116th Infantry, on the same day at Omaha Beachhead and in the same phase of the landing.

This company was an outstanding success. It started the day without heavy losses and with the unique accomplishment of getting all of its living members and all their equipment across the beach. The word "unique" means exactly that. No other infantry company at Omaha did that well in this particular.

By nightfall, Company M had completed the deepest advance within the regimental sector. That is the record, and the company needs no apologist. It can stand on what it did.

Company M's boat sections had expected to come ashore under cover of a rifle company. Had the plan worked out, they would have landed on an already-won portion of the beach. But that wasn't the way it happened. The sections landed dry against a strip of coast still under control by the enemy and vigorously defended by fire from the heights. However, the sections were well collected when they debarked on the sand; the small boats had brought them in pretty much in line.

That, too, was unique good fortune among the assault forces at Omaha. It reacted on Company M like a moral tonic, largely offsetting the shock that came from the unexpected tactical situation. The company line paused very briefly at the water's edge—a pause not arising from indecision or need to rest the men. It was made so that the line could organize, and its members could look for routes through the belt of obstacles ahead and study the beaten zones where machine-gun fire (there were six guns on them) was kicking up the sand beyond the belt of obstacles.

The company commander gave the order: "Carry everything to the shingle!" It was repeated from man to man. They started the advance with that intent and they made good.

Losing only a few men, Company M crossed the beach and gained the seawall. The manner of that advance is most interesting. They made it *crawling*. And it took them just ten minutes to get across the narrow beach. It had taken Company E, 16th Infantry, *one hour*, with the men walking only a few steps at a time.

The comparison is unfair because the moral, physical and tactical circumstances were totally unlike. But it is for the very reason that Company M, 116th, had a relatively successful experience in *its first combat engagement,* and that it continued to be an exceptionally aggressive unit on until the close of the war, that what its members said of their first advance is like a star shell illuminating an otherwise dark landscape.

Said Pfc. Hugo de Santis:

"We all knew we were carrying too much weight. It was pinning us down when the situation called for us to bound forward. The equipment had some of us whipped before we started. We would have either dropped it at the edge of the beach or remained there with it, if we had not been vigorously led."

Said Lieut. John S. Cooper:

"A few of the men were so weak from fear that they found it physically impossible to carry much more than their own weight. So the stronger men took the double risk of returning and helping the weaker men to move their stuff across the beach."

Said Serg. Bruce Heisley:

"We were all shaky and weak. I was that way though I had not been seasick during the ride in. In fact I didn't know my strength was gone until I hit the beach. I was carrying part of a machine gun. Normally I could run with it. I wanted to do so now but I found I couldn't even walk with it. I could barely lift it. So I crawled across the sand dragging it with me. I felt ashamed of my own weakness. But on looking around, I saw the others crawling and dragging the weights which they normally carried."

Said S/Sgt. Thomas B. Turner:

"We were all surprised to find that we had suddenly gone weak, and we were surprised to discover how much fire men can move through without getting hit. Under fire we learned what we had never been told—*that fear and fatigue are about the same in their effect on an advance.*

These were typical of many such statements made by men in the assault forces at Omaha. They help to explain the spectacle of hundreds of infantrymen stranded along the edge of the sands while the issue was being settled by a few relatively small bands which continued on to the high ground. The day was won by a small minority of those present, rallied by a few highly inspired leaders, prominent among them being Brig. Gen. "Dutch" Cota, who was already exploring the far side of the hill when his infantry companies came over the crest.

As for the men who couldn't get started, newspaper correspondents generously described them as "fighting grimly for a narrow strip of beach." *By their own accounts,* they were not "fighting grimly." They were dead beat and their formations had become stagnant. The substance of their testimony was that they lacked the physical strength the situation required.

FEAR EQUALS FATIGUE

READING the tactical notes from Omaha Beachhead, some might say that they prove only that we had not sufficiently hardened our men for war. But to drop it there makes all exploration of the case futile,

since these troops were as well trained and conditioned as American troops are ever likely to be in the future. Also, as I have previously pointed out, training has it limits: it can never condition men to the accomplishment of battle tasks which are in excess of their natural physical capacities.

The real lesson is the one so clearly put by Staff Sergeant Turner: "Fear and fatigue are the same in their effect on an advance." Nothing need be added to that and nothing taken away.

It is an objective statement of one of the most elementary truths of battle. Yet that truth has remained buried for centuries and it remained for an American enlisted man at Omaha Beach to say it for the first time in unequivocal language.

Whether you measure the matter by the standards of tactics or medicine, the result will be as stated. Fear and fatigue produce an immediate effect which appears to be identical. The man, whether tired or frightened, suffers a loss of muscular function and has a pervading feeling of physical weakness. The reduction of function as the consequence of fear is hence effectively the same as from physical fatigue. These facts, which were to be learned by observation of the forces of the battlefield, have more recently been confirmed in the laboratory. It can be shown that where there is chronic stress from fear over a considerable period, the physiological changes are comparable to those of fatigue. There is excessive action of the adrenal medulla and changes in the blood stream and muscle.

During the Central Pacific campaigns, two major generals, Archibald V. Arnold and Ralph C. Smith, were impressed by the phenomenon that if a skirmish line was halted two or three times during an attack by sudden enemy fire, it became impossible to get any further action from the men, even though none had been hurt. They asked me to determine why. The explanation, though not sensed clearly at the time, was that the attacking companies were being drained of their muscle power by the repeated impact of sudden fear. The store of glycogen in the muscles of the men was being burned up from this cause just as surely, though less efficiently, than if they were exhausting themselves in digging a line of entrenchments.

No appeal to spiritual forces can reverse these processes except in the measure that the appeal contributes to the relief of fear. It is as vain to believe otherwise as to think that mortals can be trained to remain absolutely unafraid in the face of death. In battle, whatever wears out the muscles reacts on the mind and whatever impairs the mind drains physical strength.

Tired men take fright more easily.

Frightened men swiftly tire.

The arrest of fear is as essential to the recovery of

physical vigor by men as is rest to the body which has been spent by hard marching or hard work.

We are therefore dealing with a chain reaction. Half of control during battle comes of the commander's avoiding useless expenditure of the physical resources of his men while taking action to break the hold of fear. The other half of it comes from sensible preparation beforehand.

When a man is tossed into combat carrying such weight that his shoulders ache and his knees shake, he has lost his main chance to conquer quickly his early fear, usually his worst. Through losing it, the probability is lessened that he will make a satisfactory early adjustment and become an efficient firer, and the chance is increased that he will become either a mental casualty or a combat goldbrick. From faulty appreciation of the logistical limits of the human carrier come the loss of tactical opportunity and the wastage of good manpower, since it is self-evident that nothing contributes more to the growth of lasting confidence in the soldier than having a successful experience his first time out in battle.

SEASONAL CHANGE

BATTLE SHOCK, resulting from an excessive load on the soldier, is a far greater danger during summer operations than in normal winter operations when the cold is not intense enough to slow the muscle and chill the bone.

As a man becomes dehydrated during summer fighting, his courage flows out through his pores, along with his muscular strength. He loses his will to fight or to take constructive action. And the worst part of it is that he is not likely to understand that his sudden loss of will power and courage is because his physical strength has been sapped and that it may be within his power to check it.

Reduced to this condition, the soldier fails to dig a foxhole, even though he knows that he is in danger. The officer fails to properly inspect his position. Troops fail to reconnoiter the immediate area of their bivouac. Commanders hesitate to give orders and defer important decisions. This is not because the voices of conscience and reason don't tell them they are doing wrong, but because they lack the will to respond. In this state of slackness, the attitude of men becomes one of general indifference to the possible consequences of inaction.

Through such tests as Task Force Frigid, we have begun to survey the effects of excessively low temperatures upon the tactical efficiency of the average individual. But it has been known for fifty years that the soldier's muscle power is seriously impaired by hot weather. Near the close of the nineteenth century, tests were conducted by the "Institute William Frederick" in Germany to measure the effect on soldiers carrying various loads under varying conditions of temperature.

It was found that if the weather was brisk, a load of forty-eight pounds could be carried on a 15-mile march by seasoned men of military physique. But in warm weather the same load caused an impairment of physical powers and the man did not return to a normal state until some time during the day following the march.

When the load was increased to sixty-nine pounds, even when the weather was cool, the man showed pronounced distress. Furthermore, *no amount of practice marching with this load made any change in the man's reactions.* He continued always to show distress in about the same amount. The conclusion was therefore drawn that it is impossible to condition the average soldier to marching with this much weight no matter how much training he is given—a finding which flatly refutes the traditional view that a weight of about sixty-five pounds is a fair and proper load for a soldier.

During warm weather, under a load of sixty pounds, the man under test began to show physical distress almost immediately, and the loss of physical power, from marching with that weight, was measurable for several days afterward. This means in effect that even if a man could go into battle with no more nerves than a robot, the carrying of sixty pounds into a prolonged engagement would result ultimately in physical breakdown.

From the physical findings alone, the Institute concluded that forty-eight pounds per man was the absolute limit under the stress and fatigue of the combat field.

The William Frederick studies, in common with all other scientific inquiries into the physical effects of overloading, had the curious blind spot directing almost no attention to the fact that physical breakdown is accompanied in ratio by a decline in the mental and moral powers of men. Yet this is of extreme importance operationally, since it means that when mobility is lost because of physically exhausted troops, defensive protection is lost with it.

That is particularly the case during operations in excessive temperatures. Postwar exercises have shown us that men have zero mobility, and hence zero fighting power when the weather gets fifty degrees below zero. In hot-weather operations, dehydration is as great a danger to the soldier. It drains his whole physiological mechanism. When the all-important body salts are reduced to subnormal levels, the loss reacts directly on the nerve system and the brain. An otherwise courageous man may be turned into a creature incapable of making positive decisions or of contending against his own fears. He is defeated by his own sweat. Anyone who has suffered a slight case of heat prostration can attest to the feeling of helplessness which attends the victim. It becomes almost impossible to string words together coherently or to force one's self to take the simplest action.

I do not doubt that there has been many a case of apparent cowardice on the battlefield, wherein it was adjudged that the offense called for a firing squad, when what was really needed were a few salt tablets.

And if salt can be replaced, why not the other vital elements in body chemistry?

It would seem possible and practical that research could be directed toward the development of substances which might quickly correct the physiological changes from prolonged fear reaction.

Looking at tactics through the eyes of the physician, Col. Albert P. Clark, Medical Corps, said in 1941: "If I had the opportunity to select personally 5,000 men from the 48,000 in this area, and feed them a specially prepared diet which included increased vitamin and mineral content, I would have a small army of unbeatable men within six months. They would be men who would fight with rocks and their bare fists if they lost their weapons."

It is a challenging idea—that by better diet control we can build men up physically until they become relatively fearproof. But if there is substance to it, then it becomes not too wild a dream to expect that a "fear pill" may give a soldier increased mobility in the future—something which while not wholly eliminating fear, will slow down its wearing effect on the muscles.

THE LOAD OF WAR

AS WITH any other problem in war, it is easier to state the factors than to outline the general means of correction. But at least several primary steps are indicated.

For one, it is necessary for the modern army to break away from the stubborn idea, dating from the Medes and the Persians, that what a soldier can carry on a hard road march during training is a fair measure of the load that he can manage efficiently when under fire. It simply isn't so. Once the fighting begins, we are dealing with a different man.

For another, it is necessary that we clear our thinking about what extra weight on the average man's back does to the forces of the battlefield. Von Moltke, that generous fellow who put 200 rounds of ammunition aboard the soldier, once remarked that, "An army which marches light will maneuver freely." It is a thought worthy of a schoolboy. While true enough, it is still nowhere near enough. If extra weight on the man had only the effect of hampering freedom of movement, we could afford it.

Its real curse on tactics is that it kills fire right at the fire base. It wastes soldiers who might otherwise be good fighting men. It kills men because it cheats the man of his best means of defense.

The third step is to set up in peacetime a system of absolute control which will make it impossible for any staff, once the firing begins to override common sense simply because it has overstrained its imagination.

That means training for weight-carrying, but arming for fleetness of foot.

It means having the courage to believe that the soldier with only five clips in his pocket but spring in his gait is tenfold stronger than the man who is foundered under the weight of ammunition he will never use.

It means schooling the soldier until he believes that a toughened back and strong legs will give him his main chance for survival, but at the same time schooling the command and staff to treat those firm muscles as the Army's most precious combat assets.

There may be an objection that this is easy to say but hard to do. The tremendous increase in the weight of material carried by the soldier over any earlier period is a much marked aspect of warfare today. So why speak of lightening the burden of the soldier when the tonnage figures rise higher even while you look at them?

The answer is that this has relatively little to do with the problem. We need only take one look at the over-all figures to make it immediately clear that the combat soldier can carry only a few of the things he needs to sustain him day after day. Actually the over-all increase in the weight of war has less to do with the overburdening of the combat soldier than a general indifference toward his problem and the failure to afford him additional relief.

The records of the Makin operation, a part of the expedition into the Gilbert Islands in November 1943, have at least one unique entry. So far as I know, it was the only operation by American forces in World War II which was weighed out to the last pound, and is therefore the only source of a basic logistical figure for one man in combat.

Everything which was carried on the APAs for the immediate use of the battalion landing teams, as well as the combat tonnage in the auxiliary craft, the replacement items and thirty days of maintenance for all services, was tabulated and computed. The total figures were then divided by the number of effectives.

The first set of figures covered materiel aboard the ships carrying the landing teams. It included individual and organizational equipment, organic weapons and vehicles, five units of fire for all weapons, C and K rations for twelve days, medical supplies for ten days, seven days of gasoline per vehicle on board, and five gallons of water for each man.

When this cargo, all of which was needed to get the BLTs into combat on a reasonable minimum basis, was weighed out, it averaged 523 *pounds per man*.

On the supply ships were B rations for twenty-four days, five gallons of water per man, thirty days of medical, engineering, quartermaster and signal supply, fifteen days of gasoline per vehicle in the BLTs, and thirty days of fuel supply for the LVTs, bulldozers and tractors. When this was added to the base load and averaged, the figure became *1,850 pounds per man*.

The expedition was a little light on alligators and had

only a few DUKWs. But its strength in armor was greater than that which normally supports an infantry regiment—one battalion had been added. When these weights—the tanks and amphibian craft—were added to the earlier totals and averaged, the expedition weighed *1,921.99 pounds per man.*

Roughly then, we can say that it takes one ton of matériel to see one man through a thirty-day campaign. That is considerably less than the usual offhand estimate. But it is still such a weighty package that it is evident that what a man is required to carry into battle is not regulated by the necessity for relieving other types of carriers. Jeeps, weasels and alligators are landing right with him, ready to do the heavy work.

The fighting man could not even leave the boat or cross the line of departure if he had to carry everything needed to sustain him for one day of fighting.

It is this distinction which makes all of the difference between the problem of the modern army and that of the Roman legion, or for that matter, of the army that fought at San Juan Hill.

In our times, armies have mastered the problem of developing transport which directly feeds the line of fire. There are instances without number from World War II of jeeps carrying ammunition to men who were under fire at ranges of less than 200 yards, and of weasels and half-tracks carrying supplies up to the OPL.

Probably in the future we will bring forth an even better jeep, with stronger traction and a lower silhouette. We will also improve the design of our amphibian craft, so that they are sturdier, more fire resistant and possessed of better road qualities.

But it is less important that we make technical improvements in our combat vehicles than that we commit them to the primary task of putting better legs under the soldier.

None but a lazy mind would be content with the excuse that it is pointless to try to find an accurate answer for the load problem since troops always make such adjustments as are necessary to survival, once they are committed to combat. That means firstly that we are content to put up with inordinate wastes in our military system. It means secondly that if the dictates of hard circumstances ever compel us to resort to a sterner discipline among our troops in time of war, simply to save the nation, without having meanwhile set new standards of efficiency in the conservation of our material resources and human energy, one part of what we are doing will be hopelessly at odds with the rest of it.

Down through the ages, human nature, as it is to be understood under the stress of war, has changed very little. The pages of history, century by century, reveal examples of military forces which were led with such consummate boldness combined with blindness, that the ranks were compelled to destroy their reserve of physical strength, in the name of maintaining discipline. Under the threat and example of extreme punishment, even while moving in the face of the enemy, men will continue to stagger under loads which are altogether destructive of their fighting powers.

In January, 1809, when the British Light Division began its terrible retreat to Corunna, Rifleman Harris was attached in person to the commander, Major General Robert Craufurd. Nearly all that he wrote about that unusually impetuous soldier bespoke his respect and admiration. He said outright that the column survived its ordeal only because Craufurd held it together with a firm rein, and he described in breat detail how squares were formed and men were flogged publicly for small acts of insubordination, even while the force was in contact with the enemy rifle line. But quite unconsciously, he gave witness to Craufurd's own indiscipline, and its effect on the wasting of the column, in this revealing passage:

"Our knapsacks were a bitter enemy in this prolonged march. Many a man died, I am convinced, who would have borne up well to the end of the retreat, but for the infernal load we carried on our backs. My own knapsack was my bitterest enemy. I felt it press me almost to the earth at times, and more than once felt that I should die under its deadly embrace. The knapsacks, in my opinion, should have been abandoned at the very commencement of the retrograde movement. It would have been better to have lost them altogether, if by such loss we could have saved the poor fellows who died strapped to them on the road."

THE RULE OF SAFETY

IN *War as I Knew It*, Gen. George S. Patton, Jr., wrote: "No soldier should be compelled to walk until he actually enters battle. [From that point forward he should] carry nothing but what he wears, his ammunition, his rations and his toilet articles. [When the battle is concluded] he should get new uniforms, new everything."

These are perfectly practical rules. The only amendment that might strengthen them would be to add that rations and ammunition should be specified only in the amounts which reason and experience tell us the soldier is likely to expend in one day. Beyond that, everything should be committed to first line transport. This includes entrenching tools since twenty heavy and sharp-edged spades will give better protection any day to an entire company than 200 of the play shovels carried by soldiers. If we are dealing with mountain operations or any special situation where first line transport will have difficulty getting through, it is wiser to assign part of the troops temporarily to special duty as bearers and carriers, excusing them from fire responsibilities.

If we are ever to have a wholly mobile army—mobile afoot as well as when motorized on the road—the fighting soldier should be expected to carry only the minimum of weapons and supplies which will give him personal protection and enable him to advance against the enemy *in the immediate situation*. He should not be loaded for tomorrow or the day after. He should not be "given an axe in case he may have to break down a door."

It is better to take the chance that soldiers will sleep cold for a night or two than to risk that they will become exhausted in battle from carrying too heavy a blanket load.

It is wiser to teach them to conserve food, how to live off the countryside, and the importance of equalizing the use of captured enemy stores than it is to take the chance of encumbering them with an overload of rations.

It is sounder to teach them to worry less about personal hygiene and appearance during the hours in which they are fighting for their lives than to weight them down with extra changes of clothing.

It is more prudent to keep them light and thereby assist them to maintain juncture than to overload them with munitions and weapons in anticipation of the dire situations which might develop, should juncture be broken.

Most of our trouble arises from mistaken estimates of

the minimum need. In training, we are overindulgent of the American soldier, and when we get ready to mount an operation, we are overfearful of what *may* happen to him. The result is that the very measures which are intended to effect an economy of men's powers help to destroy them By continually taking counsel of our fears, we in fact transfer those fears to the brain of the front-line fighter with every unnecessary pound which we load on his back.

Since in any great war of the future we will have to travel faster and farther than we have ever gone before, it is a good question whether the standard of individual mobility set by our troops during World War II will suffice, if we are to be victorious.

The possibilities of the kind of competition we may meet were outlined by Lieut. Gen. Sir Giffard Martel, who was chief of the British Military Mission to Russia during the most critical period of the late war.

He wrote: "The rank and file [of the Red Army] were magnificent from a physical point of view. Much of the equipment which we carry on vehicles accompanying the infantry are carried on the man's back in Russia. The Russians seem capable of carrying these great loads. They are exceptionally tough.

"Many of them arrived on September 6 and slept on the ground. It was bitterly cold and a little snow had fallen. The men had no blankets. But when we saw them on September 7 they were getting up and shaking themselves and seemed in good heart. Not a word was said about the cold. Two meals a day seemed to suffice for these troops."

This was the discipline to which Russian soldiers were being submitted *during a training maneuver.*

There is other abundant testimony as to how this extraordinary physical vigor and ability to endure against adverse climate which is to be found in the average Russian individual redounds to the strength of tactical forces. I have dealt with many German generals who commanded on the Eastern Front. They said, as did Martel, that the Russian seems to be inured to unusual cold, just as he seems conditioned by nature to living with the forest, and using it in all possible ways to advance his own fighting and baffle his enemies. One of these generals told of surrounding a Russian regiment along the Volkhov in the 1941 winter campaign. The Russians were in a small forest. The Germans decided to starve them out. After 10 days, German patrols found that the enemy resistance had in no wise lessened. Another week passd; a few prisoners had been taken but the majority of the entrapped regiment had succeeded in breaking through the German lines in small groups. The prisoners said that during these weeks the encircled force had subsisted on a few loaves of frozen bread, leaves and pine needles. The weather was 35° below zero. According to the prisoners, the junior leaders had never even raised the point that this cold and hunger were a sufficient reason for surrender.

BRUTE STRENGTH AND BRUTALITY

GENERAL Eisenhower wrote of his own feeling of shock on hearing Marshal Zhukov say that the Russians did not bother to clear minefields; they marched their infantry across the mined area and took their losses.

skillfully fashioned military mechanism of all time; it was more than good enough to merit the continuing confidence of our people. It demonstrated a degree of strategic mobility never before known in military forces. It mastered the mechanics of its trade.

But the significance of the achievement should not be exaggerated. We must learn to do as well with men as we have with machines. Up to the zone where men come under fire, ninety per cent of the problem of movement can be solved with the horsepower of our machines. From that line forward, ninety per cent of success depends on will power. The development of tactical mobility is almost wholly in the realm of the human spirit, since battle remains the freest of all free enterprises. Inwardly the fighting man has not greatly changed since the time of the Greeks and Romans. Whether he moves forward or hesitates in the moment when his life is at stake is almost wholly dependent on how well he has been led. Superior movement on the battlefield is the result of good leadership. The ability to command the loyalties of your men, to learn to think rapidly and resolutely in their behalf while teaching them to do likewise, and to strive always to avoid wasting their force and energy so that it may be applied in strength at the vital time and place —that is leadership of the highest possible caliber.

It is difficult for us to nourish this ancient truth while living in a machine civilization. It becomes very easy for us to play with the idea that we can build superior military power out of superlatively good industrial power.

But if we continue to slight the importance of the human element, that becomes no more possible than it was in the days of the handloom and spinning wheel. The real stuff of fighting mobility is not to be found in the troop carrier, the airplane and the tank. It remains where it has ever been—in the heart, muscle and brain of the average soldier.

The most perfect tank, airplane or self-propelled gun ever built has no mobile characteristics or offensive power on the battlefield until it comes under the control of a willing man. And willing men do not arise automatically simply because a nation has learned how to produce more efficient machinery.

The best brains of our scientists and engineers cannot alter these simple facts. Our production lines can turn out matériel until hell won't have it, and we still will not have solved the age-old mystery. Mobility in war will remain in man, in his fundamental loyalty, in the vision and intelligence which enable him to see opportunity and in the sense of duty which compels him to grasp it quickly and efficiently.

In the first great battle of the modern age of mobility —Cambrai in 1917—the British missed their cast for a great victory largely because of the overloading of the soldier.

When the order came to advance, the British tanks churned forward and cracked the German position. The infantry followed. But after four or five miles, the men collapsed from utter exhaustion, and the gap between infantry and armor could not be closed in time to keep the enemy from reorganizing.

The last great battle of the age can be lost in the same way unless there is due regard for the lesson.

Part II

THE MOBILITY OF A NATION

As to mobility and the relation of the military transport system to it, all concerned with the logistical problem in the European Theater would agree, I believe, that we never had too much power or tonnage capacity of vehicles from front to rear.

In the early period before the French railroads were running, later during the Ardennes defensive, and later again in the advance through eastern Germany, a large part of our so-called "administrative" train had to operate far forward under conditions no different than those the organic transportation of divisions in combat had to meet. Rear-area truck companies not only carried all manner of supply to front-line forces but shifted troops from one tactical situation to another. There was nothing new or novel about this use. We had done the same thing in World War I, though then we depended largely on French carriers. It is this capacity which gives the transportation of a theater a true flexibility along with general mobility.

Operating conditions in Europe gave emphasis to another important point. The fact that a prospective theater has plenty of good roads must never be taken as a guarantee that Communications Zone transportation may not undergo a heavy strain. The march of armies soon destroys any but the best road surfaces and this, by slowing up the organic transport, puts unexpected demands on the rear. And more important still, from the start the enemy attacks the sensitive points of the highway system. He knocks out bridges, tunnels, causeways, etc., to establish a series of roadblocks and force emergency detours. In wet season or winter this will choke the forward movement of supply if any sizable part of theater motorization is limited to travel on roads. The worst blocks occur on what were once good roads before they were pounded apart by field operations. That was our experience in western Europe during the two World Wars.

The lesson to be drawn from this fact is not that rear transport needs to adopt stronger track-laying vehicles in any part, even to support operations along a general front similar to those which the Third Army experienced at Metz in 1944. What we had then was in general good enough, even in the largest battle emergencies. But it would be a reckless experiment and an unjustifiable economy to reduce the standards of performance for rear-area overseas transport below the requirements of World War II.

THE WASTAGE OF POWER

But we could most certainly get along with fewer vehicles in the rear area if we would only grasp the situation by its real handle and begin now to set up policies to prevent a prodigal wastage of American manpower and supply. This was our main vice in the European Theater and in our World War II organization generally. In actual goods we wasted more materiel in western Europe in getting from Normandy Beach to the Elbe River than the two million men of the original AEF required throughout its operation. The total *requirements* of the first AEF were several million tons less than the *surplus* of the second expedition of 1944-45.

At risk of making my statements too general, I give it as my judgment that such tremendous waste came mainly from two faults in the system. The first is our over-indulgent attitude toward our troops; we seem to feel that their loyalties cannot be commanded unless the Army acts as a pappy to them and puts their creature comforts above all else. The second was a basic weakness in the checks or controls over the supply demands of the field armies. It is impossible to say which of these evils—and they are still present in the logistical thought of every service—was in the long run the more unmilitary, the more encumbering and the more extravagant. Both come, however, from the illusion that American resources are practically inexhaustible. That idea of the national wealth, and how we should use it when war comes, is by no means confined to the armed services. But to the extent that they follow this public fancy, instead of determining a fundamental soundness for their own economy, they sanction the bogging down of true mobility under unsupportable weights.

In war, all effort, all policy, should be directed toward speedier delivery of a greater volume of a more efficient fire at the decisive point. Nothing else wins in the end. It is impossible to have an efficient fighting front when the rear is extravagant and logistically unsound. The consequence of burdening communication lines with mountainous quantities of nonessential matériel can only be and must ever be that less fire is delivered upon the enemy. A lean and strong-going rifleman cannot spring fully armed and ready from the brow of an army that is elsewhere rolling in fat.

OLD MAN OF THE SEA

OVERLOADING has always been the curse of armies. Today we stagger along under a burden of soft drink machines, mammy singers and lollypops. In Wellington's time, it was the soldiers' wives and the regimental women which hindered movement.

While a prisoner in Spain, Baron Lejuene penned this arresting picture of military impedimenta in his time:

"First came the captain in his scarlet uniform, mounted on a very fine horse and carrying a big open parasol.

"Then came his wife in a pretty costume, with a very small straw hat, seated on a mule, holding up an umbrella and caressing a little black and tan King Charles spaniel on her knee, whilst she led by a blue ribbon a tame goat, which was to supply her night and morning with cream for her cup of tea.

"Beside madam walked an Irish nurse, carrying slung across her shoulder a bassinet made of green silk, in which reposed an infant, the hope of the family.

"Behind madam's mule stalked a huge grenadier, the faithful servant of the captain, with his musket over his shoulder, urging on with a stick the long-eared steed of his mistress.

"Behind him again came a donkey laden with the voluminous baggage of the family, surmounted by a tea-kettle and a cage full of canaries, whilst a jockey or groom in livery brought up the rear, mounted on a sturdy English horse, with its hide gleaming like polished steel. This groom held a huge posting whip in one hand, the cracking of the lash of which made the donkey mend its pace, and at the same time kept order among the four or five spaniels and greyhounds which served as scouts to the captain during the march of his small cavalcade."

An absurd picture, certainly. But hardly more ridiculous than the look of the United States Army when it moves abroad loaded with all of the comforts and gadgets of home. The absurdity of any unnecessary encumbrance to military movement is less a question of its nature than of its ultimate effect, and the failure of a system to take cognizance of it. In Wellington's time, it was bassinets, goats and canaries. But in the crisis of the Ardennes Battle, 1944, one requisition received in Washington covering "emergency supplies" for the ETO specified so many cases of Pond's skin cream, so many gross of brassieres and so many hand organs for religious services.

T. E. Lawrence once wrote that, "the invention of bully beef has modified land war more profoundly than the invention of gunpowder" because "range is more to strategy than force." But somehow Lawrence missed the main point—that any such advantage pressed to its extreme inevitably recoils against those who possess it. As J. F. C. Fuller wrote me in a letter a while back, "Canning in all of its many forms has become a vertible danger to military forces, the very reverse of what Lawrence meant."

When any improved method is brought forward by the civilian economy, such as a highly mobile type of refrigerating unit, the military establishment takes it up, irrespective of the factor of increased initial weight, and unmindful of the ultimate cost in load and in dollars through the availing of a more luxurious standard of field fare. Even in the field, and excepting only at the height of combat, there is not an Army mess that does not put out far more food than soldiers need for their physical well-being. This simply reflects the prodigal tendencies elsewhere in our society. The modern military commander is no more likely to adhere to self-denial as a principle which makes for success in warfare than is the top administrator in any other field. He feels that he would be tabbed as a moss-backed reactionary if he were to accept any other motto than "nothing but the best possible."

It was approximately at the time that Baron Lejeune was expressing his sarcasms concerning the petticoat influence on military movement that the tidal change began in military food supply. Among western armies, the "canning" of the wife occurred coincidentally with the very real canning of food. About 1802, Napoleon offered a substantial prize to anyone who could discovery a way of preserving meat. He was looking for a way to speed up military movement, and his immediate object was to eliminate the huge herds of cattle which until then had been driven behind the armies to provide beef.

The prize was won by Francois Alpert who invented a glass container not unlike that used by the modern housewife during the canning season. Out of his invention came the canning industry which got a tremendous boost during the American Civil War. From those techniques which enable us to preserve all manner of foodstuffs for an indefinite period come most of the luxuries and high living standards which add increasingly to the load of modern military forces while contributing little or nothing to their fighting power.

THE RUSSIAN PICTURE

IN THIS connection, it should be instructive to take one more look at the Russian. The point has already been made that as an individual, he is physically rugged and therefore a great weight carrier. Nonetheless, he carries no surplus into battle. Except for the black bread in his pack, he takes nothing into combat except weapons, ammunition and that minimum of clothing which will enable him to survive.

At his back is an Army which travels lighter than any army of modern times. True, its field forces have sometimes given foreign observers the feeling that they were heavy laden, but that was mainly because they packed along so much of the supply that western armies commonly store in their advance depots. This gives them additional operating independence of their rear, which is in itself a form of mobility. The fact is that the Soviet Command has always cut its supply requirements to a minimum, refusing to transport anything which might be obtained in the zone of engagement. The Russian Army has almost no repair shops or maintenance units of its own at the front. It carries along no heavy equipment to provide laundering service in the field. When repairs are needed to keep the Army going, local civilians are impressed for that service. Women are rounded up from the countryside by riflemen and compelled to do the Army's washing, such as it is. To delouse the clothing of troops, the Russians simply cut the cover of an empty gasoline drum, make holes in it, put a few bricks in the bottom of the drum, pour water into it, kindle a fire underneath, lay the clothing out on iron bars across the top of the drum, and drape a field blanket over the clothing to keep the steam in.

Whereas the supply discipline of the United States Army is regulated by the pressure to give troops the maximum possible of the comforts which the middle-class American has learned to expect, the Russian Army, composed in the main of men who have lived hard in their civilian environment, can operate in war on a minimum subsistence level without making its people feel abused.

As the Quartermaster General M. F. Kerner has pointed out, this means that the Communists have a relatively simple logistical problem, despite that we commonly think of the transportation of supply as being the weak link in the Soviet military system.

Many of Kerner's revelations about how they improvise in the supply and technical field are highly significant. He continues:

"In my own experience I almost never saw a Russian military truck driver with the equipment to repair his tires. Hundreds of times I have watched these drivers patch up their punctures with the help of an empty oil can, a piece of crude rubber and the help of a heavy stone from the roadside. Piercing the upper part of the can, they filled the bottom with gasoline. Then they cleaned the tire tube, laid the crude rubber patch over the hole, and placed the stone on top. By setting fire to the gasoline, the patch was vulcanized to the tube in ten minutes.

"Fuel for the tanks was usually stored in huge cast-iron drums on trailers attached to the tanks and kept rolling along behind.

"When a tank was out of order, the troops improvised a repair shop in the forest by felling three trees, trimming their branches, and arranging them cross-wise to make a lever for lifting the motor or any heavy part of the tank. Bridges were made entirely of timber. If the region was wooded, horses and oxen from local farms were commandeered to transport the trees; if there were no woods, the nearest wooden structure, whether a private home or a public building, was demolished and used for lumber.

"Russian engineers were trained in time of peace to construct wooden bridges, even massive bridges as high as 30 feet, such as those over the Don and Dnieper Rivers. In the exigency of war, these engineers could put up a bridge with no other tools than axes, hammers and clamps.

"Every army has a system of priorities for supplying its fighting troops. But Soviet transportation, controlled entirely from a central office in Moscow, had a system of such sharp penalties inflicted for minor negligence that a small delay in loading and unloading operations was treated as a serious transgression. The personnel of all forms of transportation came under the jurisdiction of military tribunals which performed their duties right at the front, often trying and sentencing the offender within 24 hours of his dereliction.

"Staff training consists, as far as possible, in pratice rather than in theory. During the war, military trainees had to study the current battles, analyze the mistakes made, and even visit the front to accustom themselves to actual combat. *All branches of the army, including medical personnel and quartermaster corps underwent this same training.*

"Little mail was transported to the front. A dilapidated three-to-four ton truck, no longer useful for priority materiel, sufficed to take care of the mail for a whole division. It was generally accepted as a mere weakness for the soldier at the front to want news of home, and the men were discouraged from writing. As in all other matters concerning the individual, the Russian soldier's feelings were of no consequence.

"Their success with logistics, in sum, is due not to extraordinary skill and efficiency, but rather to an endless ability to forage for themselves, to withstand the onslaught of the elements and to make do with whatever comes to hand."

One German general who had fought the Russians in World War II retained a particularly vivid impression of how this policy of going as far as possible on as little as possible repeatedly reflected itself in the tactical mobility of the combat command. Whereas the Czech, who had seen the system work from the inside, expressed what he saw in terms of supply conservation, the German, who had contended against this same system from the outside, saw what it meant in giving increased range and flexibility to fighting bodies.

This is what he said: "The Russian will not be held back by terrain normally considered impassable. That was where we made some of our early mistakes. Gradually we learned that it was in just such places that his appearance, and probably his attack, was to be expected. The Russian infantryman could not only overcome terrain difficulties but was able to do so very quickly. Miles of corduroy road were laid through swamp within a few days. Beaten tracks appeared through forest covered in deep snow. Ten men abreast with arms joined, in ranks 100 deep, prepared these routes in 15-minute reliefs of 1000 men each. Following this human snowplow, guns and other heavy weapons were dragged to wherever they were needed by other teams of infantrymen. During winter, snow caves which could be heated were built to provide overnight shelter for men and horses. Motorization was reduced to an absolute minimum, only the lightest vehicles being used. The horses were tough and required little care. The uniforms were suitable but the men were never overclad. Mobility came of the mass of men which moved all loads, doing the work of machines when machines would no longer work."

THE EXCESS LOAD

WHEN the Torch expedition loaded for North Africa, the troops came with so much dunnage that it was impossible to find space for it aboard some of the ships. The chief transportation officer duly reported that fact.

The response of the War Department was to issue an even larger barracks bag. In the Pacific, the men of an expedition were advised what they should carry (which was always ample); but they were not told, "That's all; you can take nothing else." The ship-to-shore handling of personal baggage was a big problem even in small operations where the main idea was to get ashore with as much surprise as possible, complete the conquest in the minimum of time, and then re-embark the greater part of the expedition. The average officer boarded the transport with a full Val-A-Pak and a loaded barracks bag. A light pack, an extra shirt and a couple of changes of underwear would have served all of his real needs. At the time of landing, whatever he carried in excess of what he needed to maintain himself in a foxhole usually became some other man's problem. Off Carlos [Ennylobegan] Island, in the Marshalls, I saw four small boats smashed and sunk on coral reefs trying to get this unnecessary cargo ashore. One coxswain was badly injured and another barely escaped drowning. That happened on D plus 1 when the fire fight was only beginning. The incident was typical of a general condition. During the last stage of the war in the Philippines, seasoned combat troops were amused to see replacements arriving laden with three or four barracks bags apiece.

ON the other side of the world, things were no different. In the European Theater, the approaches to Antwerp were at last cleared in the early winter of 1944. The first ships arrived in late November. In the early shipments came large quantities of cased Coca-Cola. This was at a time when troops were crying for overshoes and winter clothing. Brooms, mops and pails were unloaded in oversupply on the Antwerp docks at an hour when the main problem was to sweep the enemy out of his concrete emplacements in the Siegfried Line.

This lack of balance not only deprived the fighting line of necessities; it handicapped the rear in its effort to support combat. The theater piled up stuff until operations were impeded by the surplus. In the end the tonnage became so high that the handling of it from factory to front line must have cost the United States many combat divisions. And for what result? Depots and dumps grew steadily larger and more unwieldy. They were so continuously swamped from the rush of stuff arriving that they didn't know what they had, or if they did they couldn't even find it. The consequence was that special missions would fly back to the United States to plead for more ammunition or more QM supplies. So the depots became still larger and still more unmanageable as still more stuff was shipped, only to be lost again amid the accumulation.

IF this surfeit can be explained only as the unavoidable military consequence of a unique American prosperity, then it is a fair question whether our present abundance does not nourish the seeds of its own destruction, and whether we shall not reap that fruit on the day the United States must meet an equal opponent with a better sense of conservation. No doubt our national temperament is partly to blame for our military squandering. The profligacy of our everyday civilian habits is bound to carry over in some measure into the military establishment and militate against raising the standards of regulating its economy.

But we cannot pass the whole buck into the civilian lap so long as most professional soldiers who shape our military policy are content to rock with the grain. The services are not improved by the tendency to accept with little question outside counsel on all prime matters of service efficiency. There is no substitute for generalship in its real sense. The goal is still to be reached only by contending vigorously for a system of thought and action that will enable our forces to travel light, hit hard and keep on going. The lack of a fundamental supply discipline in all ranks of all the services causes more friction and destroys more mobility in the operations of American forces than any other weakness. And it is a chief contributor to our *moral* weakness.

NATURE OF THE SOLDIER

NO soldier worth his salt is afraid of sleeping cold for a night or two. No good man will become mutinous if he has to go hungry for a day. Not one would collapse of shame if enemy wire ripped out the seat of his pants and he couldn't get another pair immediately. But you would think that the life of the American nation depended on not letting any of these things happen to a single man in uniform.

When an American goes into battle he should have the best of fighting gear that money can buy—his uniform, his weapons, his equipment for medical protection and his transportation. No one takes issue with that. But beyond this fundamental requirement is where the waste comes in. In my opinion, the cry that nothing is too good for the American soldier has been shouted so long that the ear simply cannot register that too much of everything may be entirely too bad for him. For it is a rule of nature that soft handling softens men, and the rule applies not only to the combat line but to the forces supporting it.

And it is neither economically nor morally sound to make any distinction between front and rear in this respect, or go on the theory that administrative forces need extra advantages to relieve them from boredom. That belief is only a sign that we are slack both in leadership and logistics. To coddle men is to make mollycoddles of them. To give them useful work to do and use intelligence in keeping them at it is to bring out the best that is in them. So long as men are treated with respect and dignity, they will find and rejoice in a new sense of unity with new companions, and this will become ·a stronger feeling than that of missing their old associations. This is the basis of moral integrity in military forces. All ideas bearing on the treatment of troops should be shaped around it.

THE main problem is how to make ourselves sound logistically. Revolutionary thinking or not, we can only do this by working to make an army that prides itself on its ruggedness and puts personal strength above personal comfort. By so doing, the Army could play a main part in turning the nation toward the salvation it appears to be forgetting. At no time in history has any civilization or any form of government successfully protected itself without toughening its own fibers. Our future course is not likely to prove our own nation an exception.

The dilemma for the Army is obvious. If its ranks are to be filled during peace, it must compete with what civilian life has to offer. But it is also obligated to answer squarely whether the terms of the competition do not surely risk the failure of its ultimate military assignment. General Weygand, called by the French Cabinet to restore the national defenses along the line of the Somme, after the German advance to the Channel in 1940, looked his army over and then reported back to his political superiors that it was too late, that the policies which the government had sponsored for twenty years had sapped his men of courage. But when he himself had been Chief of Staff before General Gamelin was, he had not cried out against the moral decline.

Today it may sound like heresy to suggest that the policies established to dangle security in front of the soldier, and set each man up as a specialist with definitely limited obligations—and the substitution of civilian theories on personnel management for the traditional military ideals of duty and discipline—also tend to turn the Army further away from any male purpose.

THE DOG'S FAULT

THERE is the old stand-by excuse that the tail is wagging the dog. Soldiers complain that we weaken the moral drive of combat forces because of what has to be done to stimulate, or placate, the supporting establishment. But isn't it possible that it has been partly the dog's fault all along? In World War II the combat formations were wet-nursed through their training periods by service troops. Their garbage was hauled for them, their areas were policed and their latrines cleaned by someone else—this on the theory that it saved them precious time to devote to their weapons and the arts of maneuver. But did it actually make them better and more self-reliant men?

In World War I, though training may have been crude and inefficient in some respects, it at least maintained the dignity of all soldiers at a common level, irrespective of branch. In World War II, the training doctrine brought about an almost absolute grade separation between the forces of front and rear. This was done to achieve concentration of effort. But against the possible benefits of that policy, no one weighed the loss of moral strength to the general establishment which came of the failure to put one idea foremost in the indoctrination of all service troops: "You are a soldier and your final duty is to fight, and you may well have to." Instead, we tried to inspire the files of the rear by telling them that if they didn't shell peas or lay asphalt by the numbers, they would let the fighting man down. This was no higher call than that made to the ranks of union labor in the war plants. Leadership degenerated into clerkship through a large part of the rear establishments. When these same men were hastily converted into riflemen during the emergency of the 1944-45 winter, many of them acted as if they had been betrayed by their country. Some cracked up mentally on getting word that they had been drafted for front-line duty, and had to be hospitalized. Combat was as far from their thinking as a flight to Mars.

THE moral wastage that came of spoiling men by a questionable training doctrine was paralleled by the material wastage that resulted from spoiling generals by too much prosperity. The results were concomitant and reciprocal. There will always be material loss when the moral values are neglected. And indifference to the value of property is ever a spur to moral decline.

And what we made of ourselves in training was reflected in combat in all particulars. Requisitions from the front were both sent and accepted without any reference to what the soldier actually needed. Often they were a mere multiplying of the catalog by the numerical strength of the command. The cancellation of an order by higher authority was almost unheard of. Rarely if ever was anyone taken to task for having too much stuff up front at a regimental or divisional dump. But the waste up there was in ratio to the waste in the rear areas; and all because of excessive fears that somebody somewhere would run out of this or that, and the whole Army would then go to pot.

The consequence of this attitude is that there is a drag all along the line from the cantonment to the foxhole. One or two men get foot trouble because their shoes wear thin in front-line service, or didn't fit in the first place. Instead of finding out what has been choking the pipeline so that shoes can be made available where needed, we put an extra pair of shoes on every soldier. And to relieve his aching back he throws them away. Then he is inspected and found wanting and more shoes are ordered. Shoes pile up till they block the doors to the warehouses and overflow the vans which should be moving ammunition up instead.

IT CAN BE DONE

WITH the motorization we now have, all supply can

be pushed to the front far more rapidly than has ever been done before. But this will not be done unless we can all begin to convince ourselves that American soldiers can get along on far less and be the healthier for it and the better able to advance. Nor is this fundamentally just a problem of proclaiming a doctrine. It is rather one of developing a system of control and a standard of inspection that will make it work.

It may seem doubtful that the economy I have outlined is within reasonable possibility of attainment, since it would mean that the Army would be aiming at a target that seems now beyond the range of the nation. But there is at least one favorable sign that the miracle may be wrought if we but address ourselves to it. The two field armies in ETO which had the best records for supply conservation, figured on a division tonnage basis, were the Third and Seventh. Their averages were lower than the others. The difference between the low and high was something like thirty-five tons per division per day compared to seventy tons. And it was not reported of those armies which drew the least, that their troops had suffered any unusual supply shortage or that their morale was lower. In fact, it remains a point of special pride with ex-Seventh Army men *that they were so well supplied.*

But it isn't just a matter of what the field armies do. The rear area must fall in line all the way back. If the fighter has only one pair of shoes, and must face the chance of dying in them, that is reason enough why every other soldier should have the same cut. If he is allowed one barracks bag, the man in the rear area should not have two or three. If he is required to save gasoline for essential missions, that should put an end to joy-riding in Com Z. This may sound as if I am advocating spartanism all around, but it is nothing of the sort. The same steps that make for operational efficiency, and maximum usefulness in the average working individual, are also the chief preventives of boredom, which is always the excuse offered for furnishing the rear area with bottling plants, dance halls and all the frills of home.

IN 1918, a soldier bound for France was given an extra toothbrush and safety razor by his government. He got nothing else "for free." There was a candy ration at the front; it averaged one five-cent bar per man for the whole war. Strong men almost fainted from shock on that one great day when the chocolate was issued, with the mess sergeant standing guard to see that no soldier swiped an extra piece.

Did the American male change so greatly between

wars that he might have failed in combat but for the stack of goodies in the dugout mess? I don't think so. He was glad enough to have an occasional candy bar when he could get it. But surfeiting him with candy bars when he was hurting for fresh meat and fresh bread didn't make him a better soldier or enhance his appreciation of service efficiency. There were no lollipops in the early Central Pacific operations. Men fought on K rations, C rations and lukewarm water. Yet morale was as high as I have ever seen it in the Army. That is the human nature of it. Troops will never miss what they don't expect, and basically, they don't expect much. They will keep on to the limit if they get an even break with other men along the line. They will become stronger in the measure that their strength is tested.

IN emphasis I cannot do better than quote what a young American reservist who commanded an infantry battalion in Burma once wrote me in explanaiton of why his people had continued to prosper:

> We went to Burma with both woolen and khaki uniforms. You know which ones we threw away.
>
> Gas masks, mosquito bars and blankets we carried around the world, only to discard them in the first Burmese village.
>
> The jungle hammock was issued but never slept in. Can you picture an infantryman on perimeter defense worrying about getting into a jungle hammock?
>
> Our uniform was generally a T-shirt, shorts, fatigue pants, socks, shoes and maybe a helmet, maybe not, depending upon the man.
>
> Beer and whiskey were rationed to the "Calcutta Commandos." We had none and expected none.

I never heard one man complain because we had no luxuries. In the situation we faced, all recognized that plain food and ammunition were the priority items.

Our morale was high, though we saw few USO shows, and Special Service could do little for us.

We took pride in doing it the hard way. Those were the greatest days I ever knew in the Army.

TWO Ms IN MOVEMENT

AN old saying has it that mobility is a state of mind. But if we were to let it go at that, we would be no closer to knowing *what* state of mind is most conducive to decisive movement against enemy forces. So we must ask: What did Frederick and Marlborough have in common with the late General Patton?

I maintain that a careful comparison of their campaigns and command systems would reveal at least this common denominator—that they achieved their most brilliant successes by believing that willingness to take a chance would usually pay off, presupposing a level judgment of the problem. They were not cautious men. Such talents as they could apply to any situation were rarely wasted through any lack of courage. These commanders transmitted this moral attitude in turn to a determining number of men among their subordinates. That was the really important thing. They were articulate. They expressed their ideas clearly, confidently and forcefully. So doing, they supplied dynamic proof that it is always possible to quickly mold the thought and action of many through the force of one man. The lesson is clear that armies in all ages are susceptible to reform if given a clear view of the subject.

Even so, this was only half the secret. In each of these commanders the moral willingness to make a superb gamble was inseparably linked with the determination to eliminate every material impediment to movement. What they willed they first made possible. The moral and material solutions were reached together. Marlborough's phenomenally rapid marches resulted from innovations in his supply system which enabled his men to conserve their powers. Frederick, though he talked little of mobility, built a new tactical order upon a reform within the Prussian supply system. He rearranged his depots and changed his method of provisioning to lighten the load of marching forces. To other generals he said: "Your first precaution should be to *control* your own subsistence; then you can undertake anything."

In modern war the supply problem is a hundredfold more complex than anything Frederick knew. The greater size of armies and the extension of communications have made it so. It might therefore be doubted that there is still today a connection as direct between the general's state of mind and his ability to mobilize the rear so that he will gain freedom of movement. But the principle is as sound as ever, and the courageous exercise of the will is just as decisive now as it was in the centuries when every army moved by muscle power. There are two strongly contrasting illustrations of this from Operation Overlord.

GOING into Normandy, First Army was aware that it would take heavy losses in organic fighting equipment such as mortars and machine guns during the first hard struggle to get across the beaches and establish a base inland. This added stress to an already overstrained situation. The logistical establishment in England came up with a solution of the problem. It proposed to have the replacement matériel ready on the south shore of England with airplane carriers standing by to make the haul. But this was a new and untried way, and the staff worried that the stuff might not get there at the hour when it would be needed. So the plan was rejected and the extra burden of replacement matériel was loaded onto units already sagging under the weight they carried.

Two months later Third Army was awaiting the go signal for the attack into Brittany. On the day before the advance, General Patton was visited by Generals Lord, Stratton and Eyster of Communications Zone. They wanted to know how he was set as to supply and what he would expect of the rear establishment. He said, "Gentlemen, I've got three days of POL, ammunition and food. That's all we need for the start. It's up to you back there to get the rest of it up to me." He then outlined the operation as he expected it to develop. Brittany was to be cut off. One flank was to turn toward Brest, and the other was to advance on and over the Loire River. In short, he foresaw that his army would be in continuous motion for at least three weeks. The records show that he made the shot just about as he called it. His critics sometimes say of Patton that he did not know logistics and that this was his handicap. That is at best a negative truth. What he didn't know about the supply problem never slowed the movement of his armies. He respected the controlling principle. He would not overload his own forces. He demanded all the support that could be had from those who were in position to help them along. He may have missed a tree here and there but he kept his eyes on the forest.

When he got to Verdun in early September, it sometimes happened that the supply planes supporting the Third Army had to hold the air for an hour or so above the scene while engineer troops cleared away the enemy mines and otherwise tidied up the fields that were to be used for landing strips. This was mobility in the midtwentieth century.

THE SOURCE OF PRESSURE

THERE is nothing original or radical in the proposal that for the good of the state, the moral resolution of military forces is fostered best by turning from dreams of quiet contentment and the easy life to thought of overcoming of great obstacles. The late Justice Holmes was thinking not only of battle but of what is needed to keep an army fit during peace when he said: "The song for the soldier is a war song." If we are speaking of character, then it is perfectly true that whatever goes to build up the man as a civilian goes to build up the man as a soldier. At the heart of all sound teaching through the centuries, whether within military institutions or without, has dwelt the simple idea that every vigorous man needs some kind of contest, some realization of resistance overcome, before he can feel that he is making the best use of his faculties.

But we can't drop the subject at that point. The parallel does not extend indefinitely. The school of the soldier is a postgraduate course because the ultimate purpose of any fighting establishment makes a far sterner requirement of its individuals than is asked of other men. Finally, that something which has to be added—the placing of the line of duty above the line of self-interest —is all that distinguishes the soldier from the civilian. And if that aspect of military education is slighted for any reason, the nation has lost its main hold on security.

IT is right and natural that in a period of vast changes in weapon power and methods of warfare, new standards of discipline should emerge from the old. The need for a better educated soldier with a higher measure of initiative is clear enough. But the best use will not be made of such men unless the military establishment holds fast to those ideals and objectives which differentiate it from the body of the public. That is easily enough stated, but it is very hard to do.

In our times, we have permitted military thinking to become clouded by what social workers, psychiatrists, business counsel, public-relations advisers and morale experts have to say about what is proper in an army organized according to American standards, meaning the standards which are upheld in American institutions of a quite different nature. The military leader has become an unhappy worrier, confused and buffeted between rival groups of medicine men, each vending some special magic. He is told that a new order has arisen, that the rising generation is somehow different, that industrial change has revolutionized the military problem, that how he is presented to the public cuts more ice than what he really is and how he thinks, and that modern science and business methodology can rub a lamp and come up with the perfect answer to every age-old military problem.

Simply to cut through part of this murk, I suggest that

the pressure upon the Army in time of war (and in peace) to duplicate all of the comforts, habits and usages of civilian living does not derive mainly from social causes or from what the rank-and-file demand because of what they have experienced in a different environment. Its mainspring is the commercial research for a profitable market.

From the viewpoint of the businessman, and of his particular friends in political life, the wartime Army is a great business institution, and a shining mark for the sale of any product which can be given even the pale shadow of a legitimate purpose. They press upon command to accept all manner of things which it would not normally consider. Public sentiment—"nothing is too good for the boys"—moves in the same direction. That these pressures are hard to resist is well understood by everyone who was familiar with the World War II atmosphere in Washington. That they are ever likely to become less is a wishful thought hardly sustained by the passage of postwar events. In 1943, one of the lesser poets of the Pentagon expressed his feelings on this subject in the following lines:

> You said it, Buddy!
>   It's a wonderful army,
> Today our sons-o-guns
>   Overwhelmed Messina.
>
> And now excuse me:
> I have to study—
>   Gee how it charms me!
> Six easy lessons
>   On the ocarina.

The Army had purchased a supply of ocarinas for the amusement of its personnel. Then it had published a booklet of instruction on ocarina playing so that there would be less chance of the tootler being pitched on his ear into the company street, though I suggest that this last step was an error, for at least the pitch might have toughened the boy.

INTER-SERVICE RIVALRY

HOWEVER, the call for a tidal change in our thinking and method of control cannot be effectively answered in terms of a reform within one service only. The evil is rooted partly in the senseless competition between the armed services in arranging special privileges and comforts for their separate forces when engaged in joint operations. Without contributing vitally to the general morale, it serves to increase the load of war well beyond safe limits.

Consider what happened all too frequently in Pacific operations during World War II! The Army went ashore relatively light even when setting up a garrison operation. Because of the shortage of shipping space the men slept on the ground, with a blanket or so and a shelter half; they cut foliage for bedding. This would all have been tolerable if a Navy or Seabee unit had not set up next door with cots for sleeping, good housing and a ship's store, complete with free beer. (Though it may have happened the other way, with the Navy taking the spitty end of the stick, I never heard of it.) The soldier compared his own lack of luxury and skinned-down installations with the luck of the people next door. The result was the demoralization of the service which felt itself discriminated against by higher authority, and forced by the country to suffer unnecessary hardship. In the beginning the Army had stuck to the policy of shipping luxury goods only when there was stowage space beyond that required for essential military cargo. It was soon compelled to depart from this sound principle and give shipping priority to welfare goods. The load continued to increase as one service vied with another in trying to make its men feel especially favored. That we did not pay an exorbitant price for this encumbering weight was only because we were meeting an enemy already short of shipping and other resources.

The same thing would happen again in joint operations unless there were established in peacetime a mechanism for standardizing and equalizing the shore arrangements and privileges of the services wherever they operate together in war. What the Navy does for its men aboard ship is quite another matter; the rule should be equal conditions for all Americans engaged in joint service. Moreover, all should proceed on the assumption that the more men's minds are pointed toward the main object—the destruction of the enemy—the less will be the cry for lollipops.

WEIGHT AND MOVEMENT

BEFORE Grant started after Lee in 1864, he had to clean house on the baggage his Army of the Potomac carried. Sherman did the same thing to Grant's own

Western troops before going after Joe Johnston in the campaign before Atlanta. Until the very recent period of motorization in war, the great tacticians have all known that keeping an army light meant fire mobility. No one would dispute the elementary point that if a man is over-burdened, he can't move and will soon wear out. Motorization has not changed this quality in man nor has it proved the universal solvent of the basic fire problem.

During the centuries when supply transport could not move forward even as fast as a man could walk, and the largest vehicle in the regimental train was a horse-drawn cart with perhaps 1½ tons of cargo, it was clearly to be seen why the whole army had to travel light if the line was to conserve its fighting powers. There could be no shuttle back and forth, no quick resupply. Battle turned on what could be carried forward initially. Armies stripped down when they moved to attack. The alternatives were to risk defeat for want of an extra musket or else to founder.

But with the coming of the Age of Motor Vehicles Unlimited, soldiers began to think that the facts of life had diametrically changed. The possibilities of the new form of transport and of hard-surfaced road systems appeared to have no limit. The thing to be done was to gear all military concepts, both moral and material, to the speed and capacity of these new chariots. What happened? Only that the pressing danger of supply shortage which was characteristic of the era when tactics had to be based on the horse was exchanged for the evil of a continuing glut of supply, threatening to superinduce a wholly new form of military paralysis. Reversing the tale of the hoopsnake, the tail of the army began to swallow the head.

More mobile capacity meant that more supply could go forward more rapidly to troops—or so it seemed. But the end of it was that there were fewer troops in the combat area, and more vehicles had to be brought in to move greater quantities of supplies to the ever-increasing number of soldiers cluttering up the rear.

And by the hundreds of thousands these men felt more or less clearly that the duties they were doing, the time they were marking, wasn't even incidental to the prosecution of the war, with the result that many became unwilling and malcontent.

So Special Services was brought in to relieve these men from boredom. But to make that possible came more troops, more supply, more vehicles to move the supply, more crews to maintain the vehicles—and still more men to get bored. The net effect was to drain fighting power away from the force as a whole, not only through sapping its moral strength, but assigning tens of thousands of men—enough to have made a national combat reserve —to unnecessary duties in the rear areas.

ON December 1, 1945, near midnight, I stopped to talk to a Negro sentry who was walking post around a mountainous dump of medical supplies at Carentan, France, a few minutes' drive from Utah Beach. I asked him how long the dump had been there. "Since three weeks after the invasion." How long had he been doing guard duty at this point? "Since three weeks after the invasion." Had anything been removed from the pile in that time? "Maybe, but it was so long ago that I've forgotten."

And there he was, one poor soldier who had started walking around a pile of pills and bandages while the war was still within hearing distance. And he had kept on walking around it for a full year and a half—till long after the guns had at last gone silent on the plains of Bohemia.

That soldier was one victim of the system. The other victim was the combat army as a whole. We tacitly admitted that much when the worst clutch of the war came on us—when the German enemy advanced into the Ardennes. Then we began to repair the manpower deficiencies of the front by finding reinforcements in the manpower surplus of the rear.

Defenders of the system can say this wasn't so. They can say we were suddenly confronted with a desperate situation that required the SOS to make a heroic sacrifice. But those who have studied carefully and objectively that overstuffed rear will reply that it was far too ponderous all the time.

All this was not the fault of any single general or division of the staff. The SOS was no more to blame for it than the combat army. The two are simply Siamese twins. They may think with different brains but they pulse with the same bloodstream. And whatever hurts the health of one immediately affects the well-being of the other. When the front operates as if no sensible limits should ever be placed upon its demands, there will always be excessive wastage at the rear. And the thing works also the other way around. The only difference is that at the rear, the extravagance is of a different kind, and much more obvious.

There is one big reason for a drastic change in our thinking and planning. If war comes again, any one service may at some time be in position to strike the decisive blow. But if the tide were to go against us as it did late in the last war, only the Army would be in a position to win—or lose.

ESSENTIALS OF MOBILITY

HOW to cut the Gordian knot of our supply? Only by a clean stroke. All war is waste and we are by nature earth's most wasteful people. But since all of our other frontiers are gone, the Army should attempt to lead our people to understand the values that history warns are essential to their preservation. The vast size of the undertaking is plain. It would mean that the Army must contend directly against certain main currents of our national life instead of submitting to them with little reckoning of the far consequences. But the stakes are higher today than any an army ever confronted.

There is always an outcry for economy in the armed services. But the need is not for dollar-saving but for truly increasing our fighting power even though the cost is somewhat greater.

True economy within an army means that all of its processes and doctrine are shaped toward the utmost conservation of the powers that fit it for war. Because of political pressures, if for no other reason, it is exceedingly difficult to reach this ideal state. Paradoxically, it is only when the Army has a truly military posture that its political position becomes invulnerable. Its appeal to the nation is greatest when it has an assurance of inner strength.

Only by centering our sights on the target can we hope first to bracket and then hit it. A just pride in what the Army has accomplished ever invokes the need to look for improvement. It is time to despair of an institution when those who serve it, and profess to love it, no longer challenge their own system, or become less critical than those who speak with the valor of ignorance.

THE strength we need, and the objects we should be seeking, are well summed up in words once said by Marshal Foch, "We are not more numerous but we shall beat you because of our planning; we shall have greater numbers at the decisive point. By our character, our energy, our knowledge, our use of weapons, we shall succeed in raising our morale and in breaking down yours." In the final balance, whether it is a man or a nation, a mobile and successful strategy is only the result of character and common sense.

We are motorized as no great power has ever been or is likely to become in our time. Back of this transport is an industrial plant of unrivaled capacity. We have command of the seas. And with these advantages, we have no need to pile up vast reserves of supply, either during war or in advance of war. Such dead weight is an "Old Man of the Sea" upon our back, strangulating invention and modernization and preventing the efficient assignment of priorities.

In the end, it defeats its own military purpose. For when a supply system operates according to the rule that everywhere there must be more than enough of everything, the chance greatly diminishes that command will be able to put its hands on the really vital thing, in sufficient quantity, at a decisive point, in the hour of crisis. Economy of forces operates in the sphere of supply just as relentlessly as it does in its application to the striking forces.

In the age of total warfare, extravagance in a national concept of war, or in the operations of a national military system, will beget extravagance in the operations of a field division or a rifle squad. Whatever is manufactured beyond what is likely to be needed, whatever is put into the supply pipeline that might have been eliminated at no cost to the army's hitting power, inevitably decreases the volume of fire delivered against the enemy —lessens the chance of victory. Such waste of force is a depreciation of capital which, even should it not lead to defeat, must of necessity be carried as a debit into the peace that follows war.

The greater becomes the mobility and carrying capacity of an army's transport system, the stronger becomes the necessity for keeping the supply system fluid, for reducing surpluses all along the line from the factory to the front, and for G-4's learning to sleep without dreaming of disaster because he has no strategic reserve.

I N industry or in military organization, what is the final

justification for putting more money into an improved transportation system? Simply that it is the best way to forestall the waste that comes of warehousing, stockpiling and deterioration of goods. To develop yet greater road speed and dependability in military transport serves a valid strategic purpose only in the measure that it enables us to reduce the supply burden. It simply defeats its own ends if it finally builds up supply volume until it chokes movement and drains the fighting line of needed manpower. Tactical strength depends on fighting power based on freedom to supply the combat troops. But oversupply will as surely stifle that freedom as overproduction will impair the prosperity of a civilian economy.

Only the matériel *moved and used* contributes to success in war. That which remains stored is a gift to the enemy.

Highly mobile advanced bases, field bases that scarcely need to resort to dumping, ports that measure their capacity in the speed of the turn-around of the carriers in both directions, maintenance crews as adept with a tommy gun as with a grease gun—these things mean the kind of strategic mobility the future requires.

It is said that we are entering an era of area warfare, and that at last the old alignments are gone forever. Fronts may be anywhere; guerrilla warfare will be the normal order. Any link in the communications zone will be in danger of being overrun.

These same prophecies were made prior to World War II. In the event, they proved to be only about half true. On the Eastern Front, the war had essentially these characteristics, not because the Communists believe in fighting that way, as Walter Lippmann has said, but because of the tremendous expanse of frontiers and the impact of the new weapons on movement and general security. That it did not happen in the West was largely a matter of extension; it was still possible to operate in terms of the flankless front.

I F, however, the war of the future is more like the operations between Germany and Russia as to general deployments and irregular tactics, than like our own operations of World War II, then all I have said here goes double.

The more fluid the form of war, the more necessary it is for flexibility to be the main characteristic both of the machinery and the training doctrine. That is the logical counter to the increased range and killing power of today's decisive weapons. As the threat rises against all rear installations, wholly new requirements will be imposed on military organization. And chief among them that all soldiers be trained for fighting—that the rear be supplied with mobile counteroffensive power—and that the structure of the rear avoid massiveness, and acquire a new mobility.

It has been said further that we will not approach the ideal in strategic mobility until all hitting forces of the ground are made air transportable. There have been weighty recommendations that the Army proceed toward this end. We can question this on two grounds. First, the character of a national defense is based primarily on what is needed to secure the interior and its outpost line, including overseas bases. No nation, other than an aggressor pointing toward war at an already predetermined hour, can afford the waste entailed in organizing its whole national military establishment toward the strategy of intercepting a major enemy force at great distance and decisively beating it down. The second objection is that it discounts the one supreme logistical advantage the United States possesses in the power competition—the unchallenged superiority of its sea forces.

These objections aside, however, there is certainly no argument against the proposal that the more air transportable we become, the more necessary it is that we radically reduce the weight of our baggage.

TOWARD GREATER MOBILITY

THIS has been but a surface discussion of changes to bring us greater mobility. All are integral parts of one general cycle, easily stated but hard to do. To bring them off would call for more inspired sweat than any reform ever undertaken by any military organization at any time.

Always, in writing about mobility in military forces, there is a strong urge to write of the qualities of mind that are needed in the individual man if he is to be ever ready to get on his horse and go. I have resisted that temptation mainly because I feel it is starting at the wrong end.

The big need is for a more mobile doctrine handed down from on high. We need a doctrine that will reach into every corner of the military establishment—one that not only sets new objectives for our hitting, supply and transport forces, but that brings new vitality to the average soldier's orientation and indoctrination. If we can get that, we can produce more mobile soldiers, and we will not have to be so introspective about the qualities needed in junior leaders to give troops imagination and self-starting initiative. Better troops are the natural product of a more efficient examination of the nature of men, and of searching how to mould that nature to the military object in war.

No matter what Napoleon or Foch said about the relation of the material to the moral forces in war, they need mainly to be considered as one indivisible whole. The efficient conservation of men's powers, from which flows morale, can come only of an equal efficiency in the use of all material resources. That is the foundation of national military strength. There must be, too, inspired and imaginative leading. But this vital spark is fanned only when military ideals are put uppermost, and when ranks are at all times conscious that they are serving within a highly efficient institution.

EVER since the close of World War II, we have pressed research on how to develop greater power in the more decisive weapons. As I see it, this is the lesser of our two problems in the effort to build a firm security for the United States. The greater is how to develop stronger and more willing power in the man behind the gun. Should war come again, that would be the point of greatest vulnerability in our defenses. To consider well the steps we could now take might avert the very danger we fear. The well-being of any people living under a free system comes from the measures they take to keep themselves strong rather than from what they do to weaken their possible enemies.

There are words already in print that have particular application to this problem.

The people had always concentrated on material questions. They thought that the offensive power of the enemy would be broken by the defensive action of new and terrible weapons. They ruined in that way the spirit of their Army. That is what chiefly weighed in the scale. Whatever is done in an army should always aim at increasing and strengthening its moral power.

That passage may sound like a knell tolled today over the possibilities of a dread tomorrow, but it was penned by Von der Goltz in explaining why the Germans had beaten the French in 1870. But no truer words have been said by any of the later prophets. Until the day the push button at last arrives, and war can be won with the pressure of a finger, the last sentence of that quotation is ever the main line of strength for all military forces.

ONE minor thought suggests itself, and it is aimed particularly at those junior officers who have never sampled combat: All of war is a gamble and its chief rewards go to the player who, weighing the odds carefully as he moves from situation to situation, will not hesitate to plunge when he feels by instinct that his hour has arrived. The commander who follows no better rule than caution and playing his cards close to his midriff will be nickeled-to-death in combat as certainly as in penny-ante. This is a game not for fools and suckers but for those who have the courage to dare greatly.

Of necessity the military system instills in its officers respect for the high virtues of careful planning and closely reasoned estimates as a basis for decision and action. This is the main stream of all education preparatory to battle. If any other course were taken, military forces could not even conduct an approach march in orderly fashion, and their hopes would be at the mercy of the most impetuous but reckless spirits among them.

But there always comes a time in battle when the most careful planner must also be foremost in willingness to take a superb risk if there is to be inspired leading toward the decisive object at minimum most. The finest young battalion and company officers that I have ever known in combat have been men of this type. They were sedulous in planning and preparation. They made their dispositions painstakingly. They insisted on personal reconnaissance to a point where it nettled their subordinates. Thus they had at all times the feel of *their own situation*, which is half of the battle. But at the opportune moment they were ready to shoot the works. This is the essence of real generalship at all levels. It is a quality of the spirit which any man may bring forward in himself, provided that he has become truly the master of his work. But if he is careless of detail, his spirit will be possessed of a false bravado, rather than a well-placed self-confidence, and he cannot even make the start. The spirit of thoroughness combined with daring is the mainspring of action in all military forces. A good thing in a general, it is not less good in a leader of a platoon.

Looking back over his whole life in the service, Lieut. Gen. Sir Giffard Martel, Britain's great tank commander, said that he saw only one lesson: "Willingness to take a chance will usually pay off, presupposing good judgment." That says it in the fewest words. Nothing need be added. Nothing should be taken away.

Brigadier Desmond Young, the biographer of Marshall Erwin Rommel, found in the latter's operations in World War I, when Rommel was a young captain, leading trench raids and other spectacular excursions against the Italians on the Isonzo front and the Franco-British forces in Flanders, the identical tactical pattern of the movements which Rommel executed almost 30 years later on a scale one thousandfold larger against Wavell and Auchinlech in North Africa.

These minor operations, according to Young, "showed Rommel's readiness to exploit a situation to the limit, regardless of the risk involved; this led him time and again into positions of fantastic danger and yet enabled him to win every ounce of advantage, especially against an irresolute enemy." Even Winston Churchill paid tribute to Rommel in the following highly significant words: "He was a splendid military gambler, dominating his problems of supply and scornful of opposition . . . His ardour and daring inflicted grievous losses upon us."

But as Young has already pointed out, what made this general great was his ingrained habit of bold thinking, his willingness to take a superb chance when he had total command responsibility, because he had proved to himself as a junior officer that this was the soundest fighting policy.

When these qualities of mind and spirit are conjoint with the exercise of true economy in all supply operations, the result inevitably is mobility in the hitting force.